TOWARDS
THE
UNKNOWN

TOWARDS THE UNKNOWN

Memoir of a
Psychical Researcher

ERLENDUR
HARALDSSON

www.whitecrowbooks.com

PRAISE FOR ERLENDUR

NOVEMBER 3, 1931 - NOVEMBER 22, 2020

I first met Erlendur around 1996 at an SPR Conference. I was introduced to him by Professor Archie Roy, who had already formed a very high opinion of the work that Erlendur had already completed in psychical research. My first impression of him was that he wasone of nature's gentlemen, and indeed that opinion never changed throughout the next 24 years. It was then my pleasure to have him as a speaker to the Scottish Society for Psychical Research on several occasions. During that time I was able to provide accommodation for him and enjoy great discourse over meals. Erlendur's enthusiasm for psychical research never faltered, as can be seen by the many books that he has written. He was also a great supporter of others interested in the truth of this field of inquiry and, on a personal note, he, many times, came to my presentations at various SPR international conferences. He was indeed one of the giants of psychical research who has left a great legacy within his excellent books. I feel privileged to have been a friend.

~ **Tricia J Robertson, author of** *It's Life And Death, But Not As You Know It!*

I first met Erlendur in 1987, when he visited the American Society for Psychical Research, where I was working. We co-authored a short article for the ASPR Newsletter on the haunting of Höfði House in Reykjavik, the site of the summit meeting between Ronald Reagan and Mikhail Gorbachev in October 1986. He and I were interested in many of the same issues and we stayed in touch over the years following. We talked off and on about writing a book together, and eventually did—*I Saw a Light and Came Here: Children's Experiences of Reincarnation* (2016). Erlendur offered to train me in Stevensonian methods of case investigation by taking me to Lebanon to study Druze reincarnation cases, but regrettably, we could never arrange this. He was one of the most experienced field researchers in parapsychology and I would have benefitted greatly from his guidance. I last saw Erlendur at a conference in Vilnius, Lithuania, where we delivered papers on the same panel. He spent his academic career in parapsychology and will be greatly missed by the discipline; I will miss him as a friend.

~ **Jim Matlock, author of**
Signs of Reincarnation: Exploring Beliefs,
Cases, and Theory

Erlendur Haraldsson was one of the most eminent psychical researchers of his day and one of the few to have made significant contributions to both case studies and the experimental side of the field. His wide-ranging research included the investigation of mediums, death-bed visions, the miraculous phenomena of Sathya Sai Baba, and children's past-life memories. He also worked with such key figures as J B Rhine, Hans Bender, Karlis Osis and Ian Stevenson. So this enthralling memoir, his final gift to the world, provides a unique perspective of the field.

~ Bernard Carr, former President of the Society for Psychical Research

Erlendur was part of a distinct linage in psychical research history. Students of the field, including myself, were often in awe of his talks and discussions when he visited the University of Northampton, whether we ultimately shared the same conclusions or not. He was a very active and thorough researcher. He was part of a generation the likes of which we won't see again and his passing marks the transition into a new era of research. It was an honour to know him and a delight that we called each other a good friend.

~ Dr Callum E. Cooper, Senior Lecturer, Psychology Division, University of Northampton

I love you sky,
so fair, so high!
Sun, summer, spring I see in you,
I love you so, so clear, so blue!
I cannot praise enough your charms.
You hold me in your loving arms.

~ Erlendur Haraldsson, age 15 after a six-week
stay hospital due to kidney disease:

CONTENTS

~

Foreword   xiii

1. Glimpses and Touches   1

2. In Durham with J. B. Rhine   7

3. With Ian Stevenson at the University of Virginia   12

4. With Karlis Osis at the American Society for
   Psychical Research   19

5. The Medium Hafsteinn Björnsson   29

6. Speaking in a Foreign Language –
   A Case of Xenoglossy   35

7. Visions of the Dying Among Americans
   and Indians   41

8. Of this World and Another in Iceland   52

9. Face to Face with Sathya Sai Baba:
   "The Man of Miracles"   59

10. Bilocation and Changing Water into Petrol   82

11. Experiments on Healing and Precognition   91

12. The Departed Among the Living   98

13. Who Were Those Encountered?   110

14. Children Who Claim Memories of Past Lives   121

15. Two Remarkable Cases   128

16. The Physical Medium Indridi Indridason and
The Fire in Copenhagen   137

17. Research and Teaching at the University of Iceland   146

18. Companions and Contemporaries   151

19. Looking Forward to the Unknown   157

Epilogue   164

References   168

Acknowledgements   177

Index   179

FOREWORD

~

I have been studying the mysteries of consciousness and extraordinary psychic functioning for many years, seeking evidence for the survival of bodily death. During this journey, Erlendur Haraldsson's work has been a primary, invaluable resource. It seemed that no matter what area of research I was pursuing – whether children with verifiable past life memories, deathbed visions, after-death communications, or the wonders of physical mediumship – there were always Haraldsson books and papers that enriched every area. I grew increasingly impressed by the range of subjects that he had probed and the extent of his contributions over many decades to a field that was often shunned by the mainstream.

Today, I recognize him as one of the giants of research into these unusual topics, with a legacy that includes numerous books, more than a hundred journal papers, and lectures at conferences that are too numerous to count. I doubt there is any investigator or student of these topics who has not encountered the work of Erlendur Haraldsson.

Haraldsson is professor emeritus of psychology at the University of Iceland, and he studied philosophy at the universities of Copenhagen, Edinburgh and Freiburg, receiving his Ph.D. in psychology from the University of Freiburg in 1972. These achievements are small compared with the overall accomplishments of his life, but they brought much credibility to the somewhat taboo areas he investigated, allowing him to function as a pioneer in elevating the study of the so-called "paranormal" into the scientific world.

Before I began work on my 2017 book *Surviving Death: A Journalist Investigates Evidence of an Afterlife*, which brought me closer to Haraldsson's work than ever before, I had read such classics as *At the Hour of Death* (1977) written with Karlis Osis, and *The Departed Among the Living. An Investigative Study of Afterlife Encounters* (2012). I began to read the many papers and treatises of Ian Stevenson, the psychiatrist from the University of Virginia who spent decades documenting cases of young children with memories of past lives. While doing so, I ran across some stunning Haraldsson papers, such as those about Purnima Ekanayake, a young girl with birthmarks matching the death wounds from her previous life as an incense-maker, and Nazih Al-Danaf who provided more than twenty verified facts about his previous life and visited with his former family. Both cases are among the intriguing stories discussed in *Towards the Unknown*.

While reading this memoir, I was fascinated to learn about Haraldsson's longstanding partnership and friendship with Stevenson, including the fact that he was present, along with Stevenson's closest family members, at the moment Stevenson died in 2007. "He was one of my mentors and may have influenced me more than anyone else," Haraldsson writes. It's this kind of personal story-telling and reflection which brings to life the published works we are so familiar with, taking us inside the heart and mind of the man who produced them. Haraldsson shares with us the constantly changing journey of his life, putting his known works into context. And what an extraordinary life that context is – rich with travels around the world, personal transcendent experiences beginning at a young age, and the witnessing of apparent miracles, all of this occurring while he gifted the world with his scientific approach to even the most baffling topics.

Of the many works that I have encountered by Erlendur Haraldsson, his work on "drop-in communicators" and the young Icelandic medium Indridi Indridason stand out as deeply important, since I have a particular fascination with physical mediumship. Two famous cases involving the sudden appearance of communicators unrelated to anyone in the context of a sitting, involving two different mediums – that of "Runki's leg" and Emil Jensen – are among the strongest evidence on record for the survival of consciousness past death. Both of these landmark cases, stemming from the 1920's and 30's, were published by Haraldsson, and are discussed in his memoir. Without him, it is reasonable to question whether this compelling information would ever have seen the light of day.

In June 2015, when I approached Jon Beecher of White Crow books with some questions regarding some of his published authors, Jon kindly sent me the manuscript of *Indridi Indridason: The Icelandic Physical Medium* by Haraldsson and his co-author Loftur Gissurarson, which was published later that year.

This book absolutely astonished me. The manifestations which occurred during Indridi's sittings in Reykjavik between 1905 and 1909, well-documented by the most qualified and discerning intellectuals of the time, were among the more amazing of any physical mediums I had studied.

I was particularly moved by the case of Emil Jensen, the drop-in communicator who arrived unannounced one night, speaking through Indridi during a sitting to report a fire raging in Copenhagen. Jensen later manifested in Indridi's séances as a regular communicator, even showing himself in physical form. Meticulous notes were kept of all the very specific points Jensen provided about his life on earth. No one had ever attempted to verify them – until Erlendur Haraldsson took on that task in 2009. He conducted extensive research in various libraries, census collections, and city archives in Copenhagen, and was able to confirm that in fact Emil Jensen really lived. The many facts that Jensen provided through Indridi about his life on earth were indeed accurate, delivered completely independently of even the remotest connection to anyone in the room. In my opinion, Haraldsson's foray into the records about the life of this obscure individual, who appeared out of nowhere seven years after his death, represents a breakthrough that cannot be underestimated. We have the persistence and curiosity of Erlendur Haraldsson to thank for that.

After discovering his research on Indridi, I invited Erlendur to contribute a chapter to my book about Emil Jensen and other remarkable phenomena from the short life of this physical medium. He graciously agreed. His chapter stands out as one of the most evidential for the survival of consciousness in my book. I was honored when he invited me to write a foreword to his memoir, and couldn't wait to get my hands on the manuscript.

I have touched on some of the aspects of Erlendur's work and life that have inspired me personally, but there is so much more. *Towards the Unknown: Memoirs of a Psychical Researcher* takes the reader on a journey into a rich, multi-faceted and always exploratory life. Its pages reveal a deeply sensitive, brilliant and independent person of great integrity who loved adventure and never stopped probing the mysteries of psychic phenomena and consciousness, both in his outer and inner life. His goal was always to serve all of us by making his findings available. His colleagues from these endeavors, many of whom I'm sure readers will recognize, also live within these pages.

Erlendur Haraldsson, one of the most prolific contributors to an area of work that is at the core of my life, remains a pillar within that world. I now understand him and know him better, after reading *Towards the Unknown.*

Leslie Kean,
New York,
November, 2020

1

GLIMPSES AND TOUCHES

~

Most of my professional life has been spent on psychical research and asking questions about "otherworldly" realities such as, what are we and where we are going? In my childhood and youth I lived in the countryside just outside Reykjavik in Iceland. When returning home from school I would often walk home along the seashore rather than taking a longer journey by bus. Hardly anyone walked along the seashore. Sometimes the sea was wild, sometimes still. In the darkness of winter no lights lit the way. It was a good time to be alone – to reflect and question.

On these walks I would sometimes feel a great uplifting presence, and experience tremendous well being as if touched by some powerful divine being. Sometimes this experience was so strong that it caused me, to cry. These experiences started early and had a tremendous influence on my later life.

I always worked during the school holidays. One summer – when I was probably 13 or 14 years old, I was laying sewage pipes in the Seltjarnarnes municipality where I lived. One day it started to rain heavily. We sought shelter by a shed close to a pond near the sea. Suddenly the sun broke through, revealing clear blue sky, and and I marveled at how a gravel ridge between the pond and the sea glittered in the sunshine. At that moment I was overwhelmed by tremendous joy and lightness. It was as if something poured itself over me – as if a new reality had opened up – a reality which was more real than the one I lived in ordinarily.

For many days after that event, I had an unusual sense of deep joy and lightness. The experience echoed in my mind for days and to this day has never been forgotten. It swept over me again on several occasions – each time the joy was so overwhelming it brought me to tears. Sometimes it happened when I was walking alone, particularly at night while travelling home from town along the coast.

At around 15-years old I became a vegetarian and have remained one although I now eat fish occasionally because I feel my body needs it.

At that time I read *The Secret Path* by Paul Brunton and Bertrand Russell's 800 page, *History of Philosophy*. When the time came to enter university there was no question of what to study; it was philosophy. I went to the University of Copenhagen.

Aside from attending rather dull philosophy lectures, I had an opportunity to listen to the Danish philosopher and mystic, Martinus Thompsen, known as Martinus. I had already read and studied his books extensively and getting to know him personally excited my curiosity far more than traditional philosophy.

I was particularly fond of Martinus' cosmology theories, among them that all living beings carry within them a plethora of minute beings, which is an accepted truth in biology. Martinus went one step further. For him all living beings were a part of a much larger living being expanding endlessly upwards and downwards. Downward is understandable, but upward entails another worldview. A step in that direction is that some people have begun to look at Earth as an independent living unit or a living entity. That conception is approaching Martinus' ideology. Maybe that profound feeling that some people have for the divine could be a sense of a greater life, in which we live and have our being.

In Copenhagen two odd incidents happened that I particularly remember. I rented a room at a home of two women in Öster Farimagsgade. They ran a sewing and repair shop in the apartment on the first floor, which overlooked the street. The room, which they rented me, faced the back garden, as did the kitchen. In front of my room was a small corridor. Late one evening I heard someone walking in the corridor and kitchen and felt certain that it was the women. The noise lasted for a while so I opened the door, intending to greet them. As it opened, suddenly there was silence: the lights were off and no one was to be seen. I thought it was strange but I closed the door and didn't give it a second thought.

Later that night, again, I heard footsteps. I listened for a while, opened the door, and again everything was silent. The light in the corridor was still switched off and no one was to be seen. This was strange.

I slept on a sofa in the room and in front of it was a chair on which I placed small things. I had a bicycle that I stored outside, but, when I wasn't using it, I removed the front light and usually kept it on the chair. That evening I fell asleep quickly as I usually did but, after a short while, I woke up quite suddenly, feeling very uncomfortable because I was completely blinded by a bright light, which shone directly into my eyes. It took me a few seconds to get my bearings and to realize what had happened. I had been lying on my side with my face turned toward the chair, which was next to my head. For some reason the bicycle light had turned itself on and was shining directly into my eyes. Never, before or since, had the light switched on unless I had purposely switched it on. What was stranger still was that the light had moved and was facing toward me, illuminating my face. I never did get a natural explanation of what occurred in that house, but it felt as if it was something ghostlike.

Later I rented another room with an elderly lady. One night after I had turned off the lights, I saw a man, dressed in black, who opened the door and looked into the room. I sensed a clear picture of his face. That happened a few times and always in the same way. It was as if the man was looking at me and was curious about me.

At the time I didn't do anything about it. In hindsight, by not inquiring about it I missed an opportunity to find out whether any past events, such as a death, lay behind my experience. A few years later that incident would have been a reason for me to get some information from the old lady. I would have liked to have seen a photograph of her husband or ask her about former inhabitants of my room.

In April 1958 I flew to Hamburg and took a train to Freiburg. Only twelve years had passed from the end of World War II and some ruins still remained. There I studied philosophy for nearly two years at the University of Freiburg. A rich philosophy tradition prevailed in Freiburg and some well-known philosophers had taught there, among them Martin Heidegger, Heinrich Rombach and Professor Struve, who was my favourite. Struve gave a seminar on Plotinus, while Rombach lectured on the great medieval scholastic Thomas of Aquino.

Hans Bender, professor of psychology, offered a course on parapsychology that was open to all students. It was so popular that it was held in the Aula, the largest lecture hall.

Two years later, after working for a year in Iceland, I returned to Freiburg and worked mostly as a journalist. I had travelled for a year through the Middle East to India, spending some time in the Kurdish part of Iraq where I had met Mustafa Barzani and his men who were fighting for Kurdish autonomy. At that time I wrote my first book (in Icelandic), *With freedom fighters in Kurdistan.* Back in Freiburg I came to know Professor Bender personally.

On one occasion he asked me and another Icelandic student, Geir, to participate in an experiment. From time to time a man by the name of Orlob, who had psychic talents, came to Freiburg. The experiment consisted of each one of eight participants scribbling something on a piece of paper, but no word or text. I scribbled something. Bender collected the scribbles and gave them to Orlob. He described his impressions of every participant based on their scribble. Orlob was a professional psychic and, because of his special talents, he worked for large German companies by assisting them in making major decisions. His advice apparently turned out well and gave him a good income.

Bender handed each of us all the descriptions. We were told to try to identify the description meant for us. Orlob did not know who participated in the experiment and had not met any of us. I did not know who participated apart from Geir. When I read the descriptions, I recognized my description immediately and also that of Geir. Geir also recognized his description and mine. We made our assessment independently of each other.

2

IN DURHAM WITH J. B. RHINE

~

In August 1969 I completed my Haupt-Diplom in
psychology in Germany. I had then occasionally
had some correspondence with Joseph Banks
Rhine in Durham, North Carolina. Rhine was one of
the founders of parapsychology. When I finished my
studies in Germany I happily accepted an invitation to
come over and work at his *Institute for Parapsychology*.

I got on well with Rhine (not all did) and his
interesting wife, Louisa. She had collected a great
number of accounts of paranormal experiences that had
been sent to her by readers of her books. She then made
further enquiries about them by correspondence. She
conducted various analyses of her case collection and
wrote interesting articles and books on them, which
were widely read. J. B. (as many called him) and Louisa
complemented each other, he being experimental and
she concentrating on real-life experiences. At this time
ten to twelve people worked at their Institute.

Previously Rhine had been professor of psychology at Duke University. He reached the manatory retirement age in 1965. However, he wasn't ready to retire from active research. He set up office just outside Duke University and started his Foundation for Research on the Nature of Man, of which the Institute for Parapsychology was a part. He had been an active researcher his whole life, and was internationally known through the books that he had authored. Some benefactors came up with funds, which enabled him to buy a large building and to keep the new institute running. Among his benefactors was physicist Chester Carlson of the Xerox Company, who invented the photocopying technique. He was also a great supporter of Ian Stevenson at the University of Virginia, and the American Society for Psychical Research, where Karlis Osis was the director of research.

Rhine was generous enough to give me a grant that covered my living expenses in Durham. There were several research projects going on at his Institute and I felt lucky to be involved at the research center and soon I developed projects of my own.

Up to this time printed "Zener" cards were used to test for psychic ability. Each pack of 25 cards containing five different symbols was used after they had been carefully shuffled. But now a new way of testing for psychic abilities was introduced, using machines called random event generators, developed by the physicist Helmut Schmidt. These machines contained radioactive materials that were as random as anything could be, and should hence be unpredictable. The experiments were to see if people could predict or influence the random behavior of these tiny particles.

My first project was to test if people could reach statistically significant results, when they tried to foresee the results of each trial. First, I tested a large group of 74 individuals. By pressing one of four buttons on the machine, each of them predicted one hundred times, which of four different possibilities the machine would select. Through chance the participants were expected to get 25 correct answers (hits) on average, namely, to choose correctly every fourth time.

Would it be possible to reach a significantly higher result by continued testing of thosewho made 26.5 hits or more? Eleven of these 74 people reached 26.5 or more hits. I let them perform ten thousand additional trials. The result of these ten thousand trials was an average hitting rate of 26.42%. That result was highly significant and gave a probability value of .0005. In most research, such as in psychology, biology, and medicine, a probability value of .01 is considered sufficient to be deemed significant.

In 1970 I published an article about this experiment in the *Journal of Parapsychology.* The conclusion was that a few people were able to score two or more percentages over chance coincidence. However, as Rhine had found in his early days at Duke, there was no superstar among those tested.

I also played around with the random event generator and achieved a result beyond chance. I did as well as the best performers in the experiment.

Rhine gave the name extrasensory perception, in short ESP, to an "experience of, or response to, a target object, state, event or influence without sensory contact." In fact, though, we could not exclude that the participants were using psychokinesis (PK), namely purely mental influence to obtain their result.

Psi is "a general term to identify a person's extra-sensory motor communication with the environment." Psi, however, is a tricky thing: fleeting, highly unpredictable and difficult to catch. Furthermore, "decline effects" plagued the experiments; namely, results were good in the beginning, but tended to trail off. Rhine said, at one time, that the decline effects were the best-established findings in parapsychology.

There is a theory that such paranormal phenomena are unnatural and when they happen, the brain tries to close them off as soon as possible. The brain tries to exclude these phenomena, hence the decline effects. On the other hand, these effects show that the phenomenon exists.

Rhine held meetings with us regularly, and they were of two kinds. In one meeting, someone in the group presented what he or she was doing. In the other meeting, Rhine talked about some topic or told us about his correspondence with people and scholars around the world.

After my first experiment I developed another project, which I decided I would like to use for my doctoral dissertation, rather than the topic suggested by Professor Bender. I wrote to him and he accepted my ideas; to put it briefly, it was about using physiological reactions as measurements of psi.

Each spring, Rhine held a review meeting, and invited an outside scholar to come to give a lecture and resident researchers explained their findings. In the spring review meeting in 1970, the guest speaker was Robert van de Castle from the University of Virginia. He was famous for his research on sleep and dreams, but he was also also a psychologist in the department of psychiatry at the University Hospital of Virginia.

I happened to sit next to him. Robert van de Castle told me they were starting a program of internship in clinical psychology. I was planning to move back to Iceland and wanted to undertake further studies in clinical psychology but van de Castle urged me to apply, which I did. My wife, Helga, and I were accepted and we moved to Charlottesville in Virginia. Both of us obtained a grant that sufficed for living expenses. What a stroke of good luck.

3

WITH IAN STEVENSON AT THE
UNIVERSITY OF VIRGINIA

~

In Virginia I came to know Ian Stevenson. He and Van de Castle got me into the University of Virginia. Stevenson had, at a relatively young age, become the director of the department of psychiatry and had always been a prolific researcher. At that time he had recently given up his post as a director and was working primarily on research of children with memories of alleged past lives. He was also interested in mediumistic phenomena.

I told Stevenson about phenomena which had occurred at sittings with the Icelandic medium Hafsteinn Björnsson, whom Elinborg Larusdottir had written about in her books. Among these was the incident of Runolfur Runolfsson. Stevenson became interested in it and sent me to Iceland to research that incident thoroughly and later we wrote an article about it. Sometimes at Hafsteinn's sittings while in trance he would speak in languages he had not learned. The most significant example of such phenomena was when the language of the Inuits (Eskimos) in Greenland was spoken. One of the guests at the séance was a Danish man who had been brought up in Greenland; he knew that language and understood what was said. I researched this and other occurrences and Stevenson and I published joint papers on them.

By now, Stevenson was working solely on research. Chester Carlson (mentioned earlier) gave a large sum to the University of Virginia to support Stevenson's research and to found a Chair for him.

Stevenson's field of interest was very wide and it will not further be discussed here. He was interested in experience outside the physical body and alleged memories of past lives; he worked on that for a few decades.

Very early in Hafsteinn's mediumship, a (discarnate) man came through, who behaved badly, scolded the sitters and cursed. Sometimes he didn't state his name; sometimes he said his name was Jon Jonsson or Man Mansson. He said he was looking for his leg – he repeated that often. On one occasion a fish merchant, Ludvig Gudmundsson from Sandgerdi, a little town in the south of Iceland, attended a sitting with Hafsteinn. The troublesome communicator appeared yet again and declared his joy of meeting Ludvik. He insisted that his thighbone was to be found between boards in a wall in Ludvik's house in Sandgerdi, and he wanted people to look for it and bury it in a holy ground. There was a bit of a commotion and still the communicator was unwilling to give his name. Finally Ludvik said he would look for the thighbone if the communicator told the sitter his name. He became extremely angry and disappeared and, for a few sittings, he didn't appear.

Finally, at one of the sittings, he came through and gave his name as Runolfur Runolfsson. He claimed he was 52-years old when he died and that he had lived with his wife at Kolga or Klappholt by Sandgerdi. He said he had been travelling from Keflavik in the latter part of the day and that he had been drunk. He visited Sveinbjorn, a farmer in Sandgerdi, and accepted refreshments. The weather turned bad and some people on the farm wanted to follow Runolfur home. He refused company and headed home alone. On his way home he sat down by a cliff, brought out a bottle of alcohol and drank a considerable amount. Then he fell asleep and the tide came in and swept him out to sea. Later, he added, dogs and ravens came and tore his dead body apart. His remains were later found and buried at the Utskalar graveyard, except for his thighbone, which was missing. He went on to say that later his thighbone had washed ashore and it was now in the wall of Ludvik's house.

Ludvik went home and started searching for the thighbone. He found a carpenter who had worked at the house, who confirmed that a thighbone had been placed in a wall there. Ludvik had the wall opened and sure enough, they found a thighbone. It was a long thighbone, which would have belonged to a tall man. Later it became known that Runolfur or Runki, as he was nicknamed, had been a tall man. The thighbone was then buried at the Utskalar graveyard and Runki communicated via Hafsteinn that he was very happy. Runki quickly developed into the leading control communicator at Hafsteinn's séances. He would appear at every séance, play an active role in describing deceased persons who were around, and introduce them to the sitters. Some Runki would "let through" and they would then communicate directly through the medium.

I researched the story of Runki and interviewed relevant witnesses, who knew something about this case. He had lived close to Sandgerdi and had a weakness for alcohol. One day he had been in Keflavik and had drunk too much. He headed home on foot and, after he reached Sandgerdi, he had walked along the shore. It appears that he lay down due to being drunk and tired. Presumably he fell asleep, and the waves carried him out to sea. A short while later his corpse was found on the shore, quite eaten and parts were missing, but what parts was not stated. Later, a thighbone was found on the beach and no one knew where it came from or what to do with it, so some builders placed it inside the wall of a house in Sandgerdi, for good luck.

One of the most remarkable things about this case is that Runolfur first appeared at a séance where no one recognized him. He was what is called a "drop-in" communicator. These cases cannot easily be attributed to telepathy between the medium and sitters (rather than survival of death). That's why "drop-ins" are particularly interesting. There were quite a few cases of this sort at Hafsteinn's sittings.

Back to Ian Stevenson. He was hard-working and thorough in his research. He was unafraid to take on controversial topics, as if immune to potential criticism from his colleagues. He followed his own conviction. On one occasion a survey was conducted within the University of Virginia on how much academic employees worked per week. His secretary had to fill out the form and asked him how many hours he worked per day. Twelve hours was the answer. Then she asked him how many days a week. Seven, he answered, as if the question was unnecessary. This is no exaggeration.

By the end of the year I had completed my doctoral dissertation and sent it off to Freiburg. I needed to go there to defend it and it proved necessary to stay there for a few months. The German system is such that it was not enough to defend the dissertation. It is also required that you pass an examination in an additional field. I decided on philosophy and chose a subject under the guidance of a professor in that field. We agreed on my choice of Neo-Platonism, the writings of the third century Greek-Roman Plotinus and the thirteenth century German philosopher and theologian Meister Eckhart, who was accused of heresy. Eckhart died, however, before he could stand trial. He was also remarkable for the fact that he wrote in German, which was very rare for learned men at this time, who almost invariably wrote in Latin.

After I completed my orals I had to wait for a few days to graduate. I kept myself busy and, one day while I was occupied with something, I don't remember what that was, I felt as if I was supposed to do something else, but I could not remember what it was. All of a sudden, in the middle of the day, I remembered that I was supposed to receive my doctorate. I hurried to the university. When I arrived the ceremony was over and everybody was on their way out. I met Professor Hans Bender at the door. He had received the doctoral diploma on my behalf. I don't understand how I could forget this for it was, in fact, a major achievement and a festive ceremony. Only a few received a doctorate each time. I think we were six to eight that time. This was the last milestone in my formal education, but for some reason it was not deeply enough imprinted in my mind so that I would remember it.

Around that time I came in contact with Karlis Osis, who was the Director of research at the American

Society for Psychical Research. The ASPR, as we often referred to it, had a brownstone building in Manhattan, New York, close to Central Park. The society was founded in 1885. William James, who has been called the father of American psychology, was one of its founders.

At this time the ASPR was preparing major research on deathbed visions, namely visions or hallucinations that people experienced just before they died. The ASPR was looking for someone to work with Karlis Osis on that project. Stevenson had probably told Karlis that I had been in India and recommended me for the work. It had already been decided to do such research in the U.S. and in a country with a culture and religion different from that of the U.S.

India was chosen rather than Japan, possibly because Stevenson had considerable connections with doctors and universities in India, who could be helpful. I was hired to work with Karlis Osis on the project. I worked for two years and much of that time was spent in India, interviewing doctors and nurses. After that, whenever I was free from teaching at the University of Iceland, I would go to New York to work with Karlis, analyzing the data and writing up the project. We wrote a major journal paper and co-authored a book *At the Hour of Death*. It was first published in 1977, has appeared in many translations and is still in print. It became a classic in the genre.

At this point my second marriage was coming to an end. Helga was pregnant and she wanted, understandably, to give birth in Germany, where her father and her brother were both obstetricians. The connection between Helga and myself had regretfully never been very close. She was a beautiful woman and when we were in America people often said to me:

"What a beautiful wife you have." But, nevertheless our ways parted.

Regulations of airlines were such that pregnant women were not allowed to fly after a certain time during their pregnancy. Therefore she went to Germany, six months pregnant. We divorced after this, although not legally for some considerable time.

Our daughter was baptized Anna Elizabeth and was named Haraldsson according to Helga's wishes but Helga had also acquired the name Haraldsson, being born Fleischer. She found Haraldsson a more beautiful name. Anna was born in the fall of 1971 and was brought up in Germany. Early on she demonstrated a flair for mathematics. She later studied mechanical engineering, obtained a PhD and now works as an engineer, as well as taking care of her two children, Max and Benjamin. She lives with her husband, Frank Topitsch, also an engineer, close to Heidelberg.

Anna has visited me a few times in Iceland and I visit her each time I go to Germany, at least twice a year. I have also met Helga a few times. We are both very pleased with our daughter and I am truly grateful to Helga for the gift of a daughter. Helga is now in poor health and it pains me to know that. She lives on the outskirts of Heidelberg. Anna visits her often and brings the children with her, much to Helga's delight.

4

WITH KARLIS OSIS
AT THE AMERICAN SOCIETY FOR
PSYCHICAL RESEARCH

~

Karlis Osis had, for a long time, wanted to conduct a major study of deathbed visions, and, unexpectedly, the funds became available to do it.

A man by the name of James Kidd had disappeared without a trace in Arizona. He was a loner, lived in one room, and searched for copper and other metals in the mountains of Arizona. In 1949 on one of his prospecting trips he disappeared. Finally, he was declared missing. Seven years later he was officially declared dead and, in 1957, his safety deposit box at his local bank was opened. James Kidd, who everybody believed to be a poor man, was in fact quite rich. He owned valuable stocks and had two hundred thousand dollars in cash. James Kidd's Will was in his safety deposit box; it stated that all his possessions should go to research whether the soul lives on after the body dies. From what he wrote it was understood that he thought it only a matter of time before it would be possible to photograph the soul leaving the body at the time of death.

The judge took James Kidd's Will seriously and advertisements were placed in magazines offering grants to researchers who could demonstrate that their studies were in line with James' wishes. The court decided who would receive the funds. The media referred to the case as "The Ghost Trial of the Century." John G. Fuller wrote a book about it, *The Great Soul Trial.*

The court ruling took place in 1967 and lasted for 90 days. In all, 134 institutions and private individuals applied for funds; among them were institutions conducting brain research. Furthermore, some men appeared on the scene pretending to be Kidd's brothers.

The American Society for Psychical Research applied for the funds. Gardner Murphy was its president at this time. He had also been the president of the American Psychological Association, had studied at Harvard and Columbia, written several books, and was highly respected. After lengthy court hearings and later appeals, a verdict was reached. The ASPR received two thirds of the money for their research, particularly for their research on the visions of the dying. Why the visions of the dying? Because experiences between life and death might give some insight into what lay ahead.

I was sent to meet with Gardner Murphy, who then worked at a university in Washington DC. We talked for quite a while. Murphy knew India well because he had worked as an advisor to the Indian government after the disasters and mass murders that swept through the country following its partition into two independent states, India and Pakistan.

Shortly after my interview with Murphy, I was informed that I had been accepted to work with Osis on his study of deathbed visions. I really looked forward to this interesting project. I had gone into service for James Kidd, the mysterious metal miner from Arizona.

The ASPR owned a five-story house on 5 West 73rd street in New York, right by Central Park and a block away from the Dakota building, which had became famous because Beetle John Lennon and his wife Yoko Ono lived there. Yoko Ono later became known in Iceland for her powerful peace light that rises straight into the sky, which she erected on an island close to Reykjavik. Once a year the light switched on for several days in memory of John Lennon who was shot dead in front of the Dakota building in New York in 1980.

I lived in a small comfortable apartment on the top floor of the ASPR building. I liked New York and I enjoyed being among the skyscrapers. I was kept busy by my work, and did not take much advantage of what the city had to offer.

At this point in my life I started a relationship with Margret Hjalmtysdottir. We met onboard the Icelandic ship *Gullfoss* in the fall of 1955. We both instantly felt as if we had known each other before. We stayed in touch and followed what was going on in each other's lives. Now in New York, eighteen years later, we moved in together. We stayed together for thirty-two years until she died in 2005. I was fortunate enough to hold her hand when she passed way peacefully. By then we had known each other for fifty years. Margret was an unusually beautiful woman, very intelligent and we enjoyed each other's company in every way.

Margret ran a beauty salon and school in Reykjavík. During holidays and the summers she was with me in

New York. I lived close to Lincoln Center and we often went there for concerts, the ballet or the opera. And then there were the museums. I accompanied her to whatever she wanted to see whenever I had time to do so.

At that time I attended many conferences in the US such as those of the American Psychological Association and the Society for the Scientific Study of Religion. These were largely attended by sociologists, psychologists and theologians. I got to know some interesting people and gave talks about what I was working on. I particularly remember William Swatos, who had been a Fullbright professor at the University of Iceland. He was enthusiastic about the history of spiritism in Iceland and religious movements among Icelanders in the U.S. and Canada. Later he wrote a book on Icelandic spiritism with my student Loftur Reimar Gissurarson.

They dedicated the book to me. Gissurarson wrote, under my supervision, a BA thesis about Indridi Indridason, the great Icelandic physical medium. Together we wrote a scholarly article on Indridi that was published, in 1989, by the Society for Psychical Research in London, and in 2012 a book, *Indridi Indridasson: The Icelandic Physical Medium*, published by White Crow Books.

Karlis Osis was originally from Latvia. He fled when the Russians invaded his country near the end of World War II. First, he stayed at a refugee camp in Germany, then studied psychology at the University of Munich and completed his doctorate. He was offered a move to the U.S., as were so many refugees from the Baltic states. He worked in various places until Rhine discovered him. Soon he became the director of research at the ASPR.

This was the man I was to work with: a very pleasant and gentle man.

Karlis and I travelled to India together. Stevenson was aquainted with the directors and doctors at some university hospitals there and he introduced us to them. We travelled to various hospitals in the northern part of India, including Delhi, Meerut, Agra, Kanchipuram, Allahabad, Farrukabad, and more. We had meetings with staff, doctors and nurses, primarily at wards where many people had died. We explained what we were searching for and distributed questionnaires, which asked how often staff attended dying patients, and if patients reported experiencing hallucinations or visions before they lost consciousness and died.

We would then interview those who had heard reports from dying patients. In these interviews we used more specific questionnaires about the phenomena. We asked what the patients said about their visions, their illness, their diagnosis, and what kind of treatment the patients had been receiving. We asked what might possibly have caused or influenced these visions, such as medication, fever, and illnesses that were known to cause hallucinations. We collected material on a few hundred cases, both in India and the U.S.

It was ten years since I had last been in India. Not much had changed from my perspective: the same traffic jams, same fast pace and huge numbers of people. At the beginning, Karlis and I travelled together but, on later trips, Karlis had to return to the U.S. before me. As a result I conducted most of the interviews in India. We usually tried to undertake these trips in the wintertime when the temperature was bearable. By April we found it too hot to stay there.

We became acquainted with many doctors and administrators. Did they know of any people with psychic abilities or powers, such as yogis, swamis or gurus? We were aware of research which showed that some of these people had extraordinary control of biological factors such as breathing, heartbeat, and body temperature, for example in the hand. But this was purely physiological research. What about other abilities?

One man was mentioned frequently: far more often than any other. His name was Sathya Sai Baba. Some of those to whom we spoke had met him. We thought it would be interesting to go to southern India to meet Sai Baba. Karlis Osis had already heard of him because he knew a writer in New York, Arnold Schulman, who had met Baba and written one of the first books about him.

Karlis was very interested in the out-of-body experience: the phenomenon of being outside of the physical body and being aware of ones surroudings from that point of view; he was particularly interested in people who claimed they could go out-of-body at will. On our third trip to India we went to see some yogis and gurus who were said to be able to do this. We made our way to Rishikesh where the Ganges River comes down from the Himalayan Mountains. There were rumors that we could find such people there. We went to Sarnat and Bodhgaya and visited Buddhist monasteries where we met some interesting monks. We thought we might find some evidence there, but that didn't turn out to be the case. I also went alone to Darjeeling and Kalimpong in the eastern part of the Himalayan Mountains, where there were Tibetan monasteries. I did not find what we were looking for but it was interesting to visit the monasteries and the monks, most of whom had fled Tibet after the Chinese invasion in 1951.

On one trip on my way down a mountain I had an accident. The car that I was in hit a tree on the side of the road. I was thrown out of the car. The car was an open jeep and I was knocked unconscious for almost two hours. When I came to, I had complete loss of memory but, after a while, the name of the town that I was on my way to, Siliguri, came to mind and, little by little, my memory improved. No bones had been broken, but I was drowsy. Someone phoned a friend of a friend of mine whom I had been told I could turn to if needed. He came to pick me up and I was placed in his car. I lay in bed at his house for a week. I had come to know Indian hospitals too well to want to stay there.

My wallet and passport had disappeared so my friend went to the police station to get documents stating that my passport had been lost. Then something happened; I wouldn't have believed it had I not experienced it. The police demanded bribes. When I refused, they said that they would imprison me. It was getting serious. I told them I had powerful friends in New Delhi and I would let them know immediately. That sufficed: they let me go and I received the required documents. I managed to fly to Allahabad where I had friends, some of whom were doctors. They told me I was suffering from a concussion. After about three weeks, with the assistance of the Norwegian ambassador in Delhi, I finally reached home without a passport. The ambassador had previously been the Norwegian ambassador in Iceland and he kindly did everything for me that he could.

Little by little I recuperated but I was out of work for six months.

Karlis had developed equipment that was supposed to test if a participant was out-of-body. In New York he had some success, particularly with the psychic Alex Tanous. At times, Tanous seemed to be able to describe something, which was far away, which he couldn't see using his five senses, and he felt that he left his body to do that. Tanous was kept in a closed, soundproof cell at the ASPR. On the other side of the building and on another floor there was a machine and equipment, which showed pictures that were visible only in a certain place. Tanous came to New York a few times for the experiments. He was successful at the beginning of the experiments but then decline set in, as is often the case in parapsychological experiments.

In India we heard of cases of Sai Baba bilocating: disappearing from one place and reappearing in another far away. We learned of two such cases, which will be discussed in a later chapter.

I recall two memorable personal experiences from my stay in New York. Both occurred in the Saint Patrick's Cathedral on Fifth Avenue. I was ill at the time with arthritis and had to be confined to bed for a while. Then I got better. Margret was with me. I was tired of staying indoors and decided to go out to the city center. We took a bus to Fifth Avenue because it was difficult for me to walk. When we approached Saint Patrick's Cathedral we decided to go inside to sit down and rest. After a while I felt as if an invisible being was with me. It was as if it united with my consciousness. All my discomfort disappeared and a wonderful sense of bliss came over me. It reminded me of transcendental experiences that I had from time to time in my youth. This lasted for some time, but then this wonderful feeling slowly faded away. The experience was unforgettable. When we stood up and walked out of the cathedral, Margret told me that she had experienced the same, although she was perfectly healthy. I found it amazing that we should both experience the same thing and I couldn't help thinking that there were some powerful spiritual beings in Saint Patrick's Cathedral.

Another incident happened some time later. I had started working at the University of Iceland but was in New York over the summer working with Karlis Osis on our book on deathbed visions, *At the Hour of Death*. Margret was with me. This was in the middle of August, 1975, exactly twenty years after we had met on board *Gullfoss*. It was late in the day and we were close to the cathedral so we decided to go in.

We were sitting inside and it was about to close, so we stood up and walked towards the front door. As we walked along the aisle between the benches, we were both silent. All of a sudden I sensed angel-like beings on each side of me and all over the walls of the cathedral. This feeling was immensely strong: a sort of direct sensing. I could hear wonderful singing, unlike any singing I have ever heard, as if not of this earth. It carried on as we walked down the aisle. When we reached the front door, Margret did not want to go out. She had heard precisely the same singing as me and was fascinated. This was one of the most memorable experiences I have had in my life and it remained a precious life experience for both of us.

During my teenage years I had experienced an overwhelming transcendental reality and power that seemed more real than anything we can touch. The experience at the Saint Patrick's Cathedral was of this kind. It was as if the veil that separates us from the great spiritual reality had thinned and transcendental or heavenly music had reached us from the spiritual world. I'm sure that there are those who will laugh at this, but that is how I experienced it.

Margret had, in her lifetime, various kinds of remarkable experiences and sometimes we shared the same experiences. This, like many other things, created a strong bond between us.

5

THE MEDIUM HAFSTEINN BJÖRNSSON

~

Hafsteinn Björnsson (1914-1977) was the second most important medium in Iceland. Indridi Indridason was the most extraordinary medium to appear on the scene in Iceland, and famous for his physical phenomena, whereas Hafsteinn was a mental medium, albeit an outstanding one.

Stevenson and I conducted experiments with Hafsteinn during my stay at the ASPR in New York. Hafsteinn came to New York and I recruited ten Icelanders as participants. The experimental room was long, and a thick curtain separated Hafsteinn from the participants. They came in one at a time and sat in a chair, while Hafsteinn gave his readings describing deceased people that he sensed, saw or heard around them. Stevenson chose at random in what order the participants appeared in the experiment.

I did not know the order Stevenson had chosen and Hafsteinn didn't know, at any time, who was sitting behind the curtain. The participants wore earplugs and headphones with loud music playing, so they couldn't hear what Hafsteinn said.

Hafsteinn's descriptions were tape recorded and later transcribed. A few days after the experiment, every participant received copies of all the ten readings after they had been placed in a random order. Each participant read through all the readings/descriptions, and marked descriptions of people whom they recognized. When all participants had done this and had recorded their choices, Stevenson and I exchanged our lists. Four out of the ten participants had chosen the reading that Hafsteinn had given while they were sitting in the chair. This was statistically significant but not perfect.

After the experiment, it occurred to me that many of the participants were young, so I asked them to give the readings to their parents. The parents reported recognizing many of the deceased communicators whom the young people weren't aware of.

Another experiment followed with no significant results, but many participants recognized communicators from other people's readings. Could it confuse Hafsteinn to have all the participants in the house at the same time? The next experiment took place in Reykjavik and this time all participants received twenty readings: ten from the experiment they had just participated in and ten from a previous experiment. This time all ten participants picked a reading from their own experiment. That was highly significant.

I told Stevenson about a case where Hafsteinn spoke to a sitter in Inuit or Eskimo language of Greenland; Hafsteinn didn't speak Inuit. Could other such cases be found? Hafsteinn agreed that I could attend all his séances for a month, audio-record them, and bring a few sitters to his séances, one at a time, who spoke a language unknown to him.

With Hafsteinn, usually a so-called controller appeared, such as Runki, who brought messages to the sitters. But sometime communicators talked directly through him, a few at each sitting. Usually Hafsteinn touched the sitter whom the communicator wanted to contact.

Once he took my hand firmly. Somebody addressed me. At first I did not recognize who he was. Then I heard a firm voice: "What is this, man? Don't you know who I am? This is Stefan. Don't you remember me in the swimming pool?" Then I remembered a patient who stayed for a long time at the sanatorium in Hveragerdi when I worked there. His name was Stefan. He was from the southeast of Iceland, had a stiff hip but moved quite swiftly, was very strong and had a lively personality. I could look into the swimming pool from where I worked and Stefan was always there; he was usually the first one in the pool in the morning. Stefan was there more than anybody else. When he greeted people he shook them firmly by the hand, and now Hafsteinn, in trance, was shaking my hand in the same way. Then he added so as to leave me in no doubt: "They liked you pinching them, the ladies." He was talking about the way I used to massage people. This was typical of Stefan.

The incident was memorable, for Hafsteinn knew nothng about Stefan, let alone that I knew him, and that he frequented the sanatorium swimming pool. I had not thought of Stefan since I was working in Hveragerdi. That is why it took me a few seconds to recognize him, but once I had it was obvious. Many people who sat at Hafsteinn's meetings told similar stories.

I recall another similar incident. A communicator – a man from Gardur in the southwest of Iceland – connected with a sitter who was from – or was familiar with – that area. Suddenly the sitter touched my hand and said: "I knew him when he was young." This man's name was Gudlaugur Eiriksson; he was married to my father's sister, Bjorg. I spent some summers with them before the war. Hafsteinn could not have had the faintest idea that I had stayed in the Gardur area, let alone that that I stayed at the home of Gudlaugur and Bjorg.

At Easter that year I was with Hafsteinn and I accompanied him to the east of Iceland. There he held five séances a day. Hafsteinn did not have anything to do with the bookings of these séances, and did not know who would be coming to each meeting. Some people claimed that he was curious about the people who would come to the meetings and would seek information about them. That was far from the truth. I was with him and, during the break between sittings, all he wanted to do was to to have coffee and relax for a while. Far from seeking information, he tried to avoid meeting the sitters.

Our flight to the east of the country was delayed due to bad weather. Before we arrived, Hafsteinn told me that the spirits on the other side, who had lived in the east, were already "crowding" him.

By travelling and spending days and nights with Hafsteinn, I got to know him well, and I became familiar with his routine at the sittings. Hafsteinn's meetings were very diverse and it was an exception if the same deceased persons appeared at more than one meeting. A steady stream of people, who had passed away, appeared day after day at the sittings and most gave their full name, which is unusual in mental mediumship.

Hafsteinn was polite, punctual and orderly. He was not talkative, but he was an intelligent man. Hymns were sung at the beginning of every sitting and a prayer was said. It was dark in the room apart from a soft red light. At the beginning of a sitting, a blow was heard as if Hafsteinn had exhaled all the air from his lungs. After that he was in trance, and voices were heard, coming from his throat, which sounded different from his normal voice. These were his controls. At one sitting an elderly woman came through first and spoke in a low voice. Then Runki came and spoke in a loud, clear voice. He described those, from the other side who were present. Then Runki left and spirits came through directly.

Communicators usually addressed a particular sitter. One thing was evident: of the multitude of spirits that came through, a relatively high percentage had died violently, usually by accident. However, these communicators were far from being the majority.

At the time I was with Hafsteinn, he held some group séances, which he called clairvoyant meetings. They were held in community halls in the country and large cinema houses in Reykjavik. He would be in half-trance, as he called it, and he knew what was going on around him, while, at the same time, he could sense those who had passed away.

I recorded several of these meetings. Usually around 150 people were described at these meetings. He would start by describing a certain person and then their close relatives, acquaintances or co-workers: often six to eight people, who were connected to each other. Then he called out into the hall, usually to a certain area, and asked whether anybody recognized his description and usually someone did. Unfortunately, I never proved the accuracy or correctness of the communications, as the guests disappeared as soon as the meeting was over. For me, that's why personal communication is so valuable.

The mediumship was a calling with Hafsteinn. He was very popular and it was difficult to get a séance with him. He had barely any respite from people who wanted to attend his meetings. He worked all day as a bill collector for the National Radio Company. He had been employed there by the general manager of the station, Jonas Thorbergsson, who was very interested in spiritualism. He had been influential in training Hafsteinn as a medium, although his primary teacher was Einar H. Kvaran, who had also investigated and trained Indridi Indridason.

At the end of his work day, Hafsteinn would walk to the Society for Psychical Research, which occupied a house in Gardastraeti, and would hold two sittings. Most evenings he didn't get home until almost 10:00 pm. He worked week after week, year after year. He used his holidays to go to towns outside Reykjavik, such as Akureyri in the north and Egilsstadir in the east. There he held up to five sittings a day.

In March and April 1972, I recorded 53 séances with Hafsteinn as well as several clairvoyant meetings, which he held in various parts of the country. These recordings are currently housed in the sound department of the Icelandic National Library.

6

SPEAKING IN A FOREIGN LANGUAGE – A CASE OF XENOGLOSSY

~

A Danish man, Professor Svend Fredriksen, had a sitting with Hafsteinn in 1966. Fredriksen was brought up in Sisimiut, the second largest town situated on the West Coast of Greenland. His father was a clergyman there.

Fredriksen naturally came to know and speak the Inuit/Eskimo language as he grew up playing with the native children, and he married a Greenlandic girl. Later, he worked in Copenhagen. There he got to know the Icelandic writer Jon Bjornsson, who lived in Denmark from 1932 to 1945.

In September 1966 Svend was on his way to Copenhagen and stopped in Reykjavik to see his friend Jon. There, he attended a sitting with Hafsteinn. By then Fredriksen had become a professor of Eskimo (Inuit) languages and anthropology at the Catholic University in Washington DC.

When Svend came home to Jon after the sitting, he was – Jon Bjornsson told me – very excited and happy. Many people from the other side came to him, among them a shaman he had known in Greenland as a boy. That one came directly through Hafsteinn and they exchanged a few sentences in Inuit. I tried to meet professor Fredriksen in Washington in the 1970s, but by then he had passsed away.

At séances Hafsteinn usually had two experienced sitters, one at each side. On this occasion it was Hulda S. Helgadottir, who was, for a long time, a sitter with Hafsteinn, and Ulfur Ragnarssson, a medical doctor, who had a Danish mother. Hulda found this sitting so unique that she wrote it down immediately the same evening – although she had never done that before – as she had promised to keep everything that happened at the sittings confidential. Hulda's narrative was published in 1970 in *Hvert liggur leidin? (Where are we heading?)* by Elinborg Larusdottir. I met Hulda and she told me that a communicator from Greenland had appeared at the sitting and Professor Svend Fredriksen and he and the communicator spoke in in Greenlandic or another Greenland dialect but she did not understand what was said.

I knew the other sitter, Ulfur Ragnarsson, a well known medical doctor and psychotherapist. He did not know if Fredriksen wrote down his experience but he recalled his making notes during the séance as he was always writing something. Ulfur reported that Fredriksen told him that the man, who came through and spoke the Eskimo language, had been a shaman (aandeman in Danish) when alive. He had been considered a wise man and people sought advice and counsel from him during his harsh life in Greenland. He had knowledge of the particular shamanic "language" that Frederiksen was keen to record, before all who used it were gone.

This is how Hulda described the sitting in the book by Elinborg:

> With him (Svend Fredriksen) a large group of people is described and people come directly through, who talk to him in Danish and he talks to them in that language. He describes his enjoyment and I feel that he barely expected such a wonderful result of his sitting with an Icelandic medium. But his surprise was to be far greater when Runolfur starts describing a group of people from Greenland that have appeared and show themselves in their peculiar clothing that is so strange to us, but Runolfur describes it with Icelandic accuracy and professor Fredriksen recognizes every garment.
>
> They show Fredriksen dogsleds and kayaks and mention names that are not understandable to us and make Fredriksen almost elevate from his seat in astonishment. He knew these people and lived daily with them in his youth before they moved from our realm of existence. Now they have come to him on a foreign ground and in unfamiliar surroundings with the help of a man gifted with a rare talent that he wanted so much to come to know. Suddenly Runolfur remarks:
>
> There is a man here who is so eager to talk to you. I think I have to let him try if he can handle it."

As Runolfur leaves the connection, there comes
through a person who really has an errand with
our foreign visitor (Fredriksen). A joyous reunion
takes place, and we become witness to, that from
the lips of the medium sounds the unique language
of the Greenlandic Eskimos that no Icelander
understands. Prof. Fredriksen responds in the
same language and they exchange a few sentences.

In Elinborg Larusdottir's book, one can also find
a comment by Ulfur Ragnarsson on Hulda's account.
He writes: "I remember well most things that are
mentioned in your account and it is correctly stated
… I am reminded of when professor Fredriksen told
me, that the man, who spoke Greenlandic through the
lips of the medium, had been a shaman while alive. He
came through uniquely clearly."

I had a meeting with Hafsteinn on the 11th of October
1972 where I selected the sitters. I chose five people
whom I knew well, without Hafsteinn knowing who
they were. Among them were Sveinn Rognvaldsson
and his wife, Alma Andresdottir.

Four men came through for Sveinn and gave their
full names: Thordur Petursson, Magnus Gislason,
Thorvaldur Benediktsson and Hordur Kristinsson.
They all said they had drowned on the Newfoundland
fishing banks. This completely surprised Sveinn. It was
said at the meeting that they had known Sveinn. These
men had been onthe trawler *July* from Hafnarfjordur
that sank off Newfoundland on the 12th of February
1959 with 30 people aboard. Sveinn had been on many
tours on the trawler *June* that was owned by the same
company at Hafnarfjordur. Some in the crew of *July* had
been Sveinn's shipmates on earlier tours. Sveinn relates:

I had made a few trips onboard the trawler *June* from the same fisheries company and had an opportunity to go on this trip on *July* and had been registered on the trawler. The day the ship was to sail from harbor my wife Alma had a fear and panic attack and tried to do everything she could to stop me from going. She hit me and fell on the floor. The last thing she tells me is: "Go then and lie at the bottom of the sea." I go out from Alma with my luggage on my back, but I am astounded by the state she found herself in. I felt as if something got into her and that she could not control herself. She completely lost control. I had promised to stop at a house of an acquaintance, who was also to go on this trip. His mother had forgotten to wake him up. I told his mother: "I am not going." She lets him continue sleeping. *July* sails from harbor without us and I go home with my kit bag.

Sveinn had never met Hafsteinn and Hafsteinn would not have known him at all. Of course Hafsteinn knew well, like everyone else in the country, about this terrible ship calamity and may have read the names of the crew members in the newspapers. But why did these men come to Sveinn and not to somebody else? Sveinn was the only one of the sitters, who had any connection with the crew of *July*.

A sound recording exists of this sitting. After I had finished writing this chapter I called Sveinn. He described this incident to me again as did his his wife Alma. He remembered that sitting very well. Sveinn read the final text and approved it.

For several decades Hafsteinn had lived with his wife, Thordis Helgadottir, but in later years they divorced. Hafsteinn married again to Gudlaug E. Kristinsdottir and lived with her until he died of a heart attack in 1977. Thordis died in December of 1985 and Margret and I went to her funeral, as we knew her quite well. There were many mourners present. Then something happened that I remember very well, although I don't know if anyone other than Margret and I sensed what we experienced.

A certain atmosphere existed at Hafsteinn's sittings, particularly around Runolfur (Runki). On the day of the funeral it was as if Hafsteinn and his entourage had arrived and their atmosphere filled the church. This was accompanied by sound, music, and singing as from afar. That experience is one of the more memorable of this kind that has happened to me. After a while it faded away. When we had left the church, I asked Margret if she had sensed anything unusual. She described the same thing. That was my last connection with Hafsteinn and his group.

7

VISIONS OF THE DYING AMONG AMERICANS AND INDIANS

～

Sir William Barrett was a well-known physicist at the Royal College in Dublin. In his later years he wrote a book called *Deathbed Visions,* which was published in 1926, a year after his death. It was mostly based on the observations of his wife, who was an obstetrician, and had often been present when women died giving birth. Some of these women had visions/hallucinations and saw deceased relatives who had arrived to receive them.

After Barrett's book was published, little or no research was done on deathbed visions until Osis started to gather new cases in the 1950s. His interest stemmed from a case in his family.

Could these visionary experiences tell us something about what lay ahead after the death of the physical body? Was there a medical explanation for them? Had those, who had them, been receiving medicine that was known to cause hallucinations? Did they have a high temperature? Had they suffered from illnesses that can cause hallucinations? There were more questions of this kind. For every case we had a long list of such questions.

What effect did religion have on these experiences? Did they occur only to those who live in our Christian world? This was the reason why it was decided to do the study in the United States and also in a non-Christian Asian country. We looked for Buddhist or Hindu countries such as Japan and India.

In the end it was decided to do the study in India. Ian Stevenson could give us helpful contacts with the medical community in India, and he came with us on the first trip to get us going. We concentrated on getting in touch with hospital wards where many people had died. We held meetings with the doctors and nursing staff. They were asked whether they had observed hallucinations in dying patients, what they were about, and if the patients had mentioned people or described heavenly surroundings. We also asked about experiences of patients who had lost consciousness, almost died, but returned back to life. We inquired about incidents where the emotional wellbeing of patients improved quite markedly just before dying. Healthcare workers, who had observed such cases, were singled out for more thorough questions. In all, 435 doctors and nursing staff were interviewed in India and 442 in the U. S.

The majority of visions just before death were of departed relatives and sometimes of religious or divine beings. The dying patient sensed that these beings had come to take him or her into another world. Often the patients' wellbeing drastically impoved when this happened. In many instances the patients had been worried or afraid to die but, after the visions, they usually felt happy to go.

Here is an example from the United States:

> A female cardiac patient in her fifties knew that she was dying and was in a discouraged, depressed mood. Suddenly, she raised her arms and her eyes opened wide; her face lit up as if she was seeing someone she hadn't seen for a long time. She said, "Oh, Katie, Katie." The patient had been suddenly roused from a comatose state, she seemed happy, and she died immediately after the hallucination. There were several Katies in this woman's family: a half-sister, an aunt, and a friend. All were dead.

Below is another example of an American, who suffered from a painful, deadly illness. Our witness reported the following:

> Well, it was an experience of meeting someone whom he deeply loved. He smiled, reached up, and held out his hands. The expression on his face was one of joy. I asked him what he saw. He said his wife was standing right there and waiting for him. It looked as though there was a river and she was on the other side, waiting for him to come across. He became very quiet and peaceful – serenity of a religious kind. He was no longer afraid.

Our cases revealed that some patients reached an emotional high shortly before dying: a great feeling of wellbeing. Furthermore, the data showed that a great number of these patients were not under the influence of drugs or medical conditions that were known to cause hallucinations. We constructed a scale or index number for factors known to cause hallucinations. It turned out that these visions were not connected to the scale. In fact, if the patients were high on this scale, they were less likely to have visions about someone coming to fetch them, but more likely to have confusing hallucinations. We found this of great interest.

In the U. S. as well as in India it was common that dying patients saw departed loved ones who invited the patients to follow them to another world. In one aspect there was a difference. In India it was more common that religious beings appeared to the patient than people. It was also rather common that beings appeared who wanted to take them to another world, but they did not want to go.

In our opinion these cases could possibly be traced to the fact that according to Hinduism, messengers of the god Yama (god of death) appear at a deathbed to fetch the dying person to another world. These messengers of death are called *Yamdoots*. According to the Hindu religion, they appear in a disguise according to how morally the person has lived. This is reminiscent of the Catholic ideas of purgatory. If a person has lived a life of sin, Yamdoot appears in a threatening form.

The observations were more frequently reported by nurses than doctors, probably because nurses spend more time with patients than do doctors. The only time doctors reported more detailed cases was when the dying person was one of their relatives, meaning doctors spent more time with their relatives!

It's worth bearing in mind that the average age of the dying patients was 62 in the U. S. and 42 in India.

That may, in part, explain the fact that Indians often struggled against dying when a being appeared to them, saying that they had come to fetch them to another world. It makes sense that younger people are more reluctant to let go and die than older people. In India it was more common for a person to die of infectious diseases and infections after an operation than of old age.

In other ways the results were similar in both countries. We can say that the main reason for the visions is not medication, fever or other factors known to cause hallucinations. That is an important finding in itself. This is not a proof, but a sign of the reality of another existence.

Such signs of another existence are also found in the experiences of those who almost die but are brought back to life, namely the near-death experience. Much research has recently been conducted at university hospitals in the U. S., England and the Netherlands. Their findings are similar to those, which Karlis and I found in our study.

Karlis had conducted a preliminary deathbed vision study in the U. S. several years before the major study in the U. S. and India. Visions of someone coming to fetch the dying person were 79% in our Indian sample, 69% in the American sample and 79% in the preliminary study.

There were a few cases where the patient had not expected to die but sensed that somebody had come to fetch them and died shortly afterwards, contrary to the expectations of doctors or relatives. Here is an example:

A seventy-year-old patient had seen her deceased husband several times and then she predicted her own death. She said that her husband had appeared in the window and motioned her to come out of the house. The reason for his visits was to have her join him. Her daughter and other relatives were present when she predicted her death, [she] laid out her burial clothes, lay down in bed for a nap, and died about one hour later. She seemed calm, resigned to death and, in fact, wanted to die. Before she saw her husband she didn't speak about imminent death. Her doctor was so surprised by her sudden death, for which there were no sufficient medical reasons, that he checked if she had poisoned herself. He found neither signs of poisoning nor any such drugs in the house.

Here are additional examples of a patient who sees a vision just before dying:

A 68-year-old Polish housewife was afflicted with cancer. Her mind was clear. She was settling some financial matters and asked for her purse. She had not thought of dying. Then she saw her husband who had died twenty years before. She was happy, with a sort of religious feeling and, according to her doctor, she lost all fear of death. Instead of fearing death, she felt it to be the logical, correct thing. She died within 5 or 10 minutes.

An Indian physician in a Muslim hospital reported the following case:

A male patient in his fifties, college educated and a Christian, was going to be discharged on the seventh day after an operation on a fractured hip. The patient was without fever and not receiving any sedation. Then he developed chest pain and I was called to him. When I came he told me he was going to die. "Why do you say so? Having a little pain in the chest does not mean you are going to die." Then the patient told how immediately after the pain in the chest started he had had a hallucination, but still remained [in] his full consciousness. He said he felt himself for a few seconds to be not in this world but elsewhere. At that time he saw Christ coming down through the air very slowly. Christ called him, rather, waved his hand that he should come to him. Then Christ disappeared and he was fully here. The patient told me he would die within a few minutes. He seemed quite happy and said that the aim of his life had been achieved by Christ calling him to Him. "I am going," he said, and departed a few minutes later.

In the following case, Yamdoot appeared to a Hindu clerical worker, high school educated, who was hospitalized with an infectious disease. His temperature was high, he was mildly affected by drugs, but, to his nurse, his consciousness seemed to be clear when he exclaimed:

"Somebody is standing there! He has a cart with him so he must be a Yamdoot! He must be taking someone with him. He is teasing me that he is going to take me! But, Mamie, I am not going; I want to be with you!" Then he said someone was pulling him out of bed. He pleaded, "Please hold me; I am not going." His pain increased and he died.

Finally here is an example of a ten-year-old girl in a hospital in Pennsylvania recovering from pneumonia. Her temperature had subsided, and she seemed to be past the crisis.

The mother saw that her child seemed to be sinking and called us [nurses]. She said that the child had just told her she had seen an angel who had taken her by the hand – and she was gone, died immediately. That just astounded us because there was no sign of imminent death. She was so calm and serene – and so close to death!

Analyzing the data and writing *At The Hour of Death* was a great deal of work. When it was finished we looked for a publisher. We got lots of rejections. Finally, when we were about to give up, we found Avon books, a large publishing company. The book sold well, and even got on one bestseller list for a short while. Soon, requests of translations followed and it was translated into German, French, Dutch, Italian, Spanish, Portuguese, Swedish, Norwegian, Icelandic, Japanese, Persian and Malayalam, the language spoken in Kerala, India.

The book received a few reviews, most of them positive. David H. Ingvar, a professor in clinical neurophysics at the University of Lund, wrote one critical review in *Sydsvenska Dagbladed* after our book was published in Swedish. He claimed that these visions were caused by lack of oxygen and affirmed that such visions could be produced in healthy people by reducing oxygen flow to the brain. Airline pilots in high altitude had similar experiences, when they lacked oxygen.

I wrote to him and asked for sources, but only got the answer that in experiments with various levels of oxygen, hallucinations could appear on the edge of the visual field. He pointed out the laboratories of the U. S. Air Force, but could not give an address. Further correspondence led to his giving me a name of a doctor, who should know more. His name was Carl Wilhelm Sem-Jacobsen; he worked at the Gaustad hospital in Oslo. He was very friendly and pointed out an old friend of his, James C. Culver, who was the head of The Air Force School of Aviation and Space Medicine in San Antonio, Texas. He would be best qualified to give me the information I needed. This Culver – commander-in-chief was his title – reacted well to my request and had people search in the database of his organization for sources on the potential effect of lack of oxygen on hallucination. His answer dated the 8th of May 1981 was the following: "The Aeromedical Library of the USAF School of Aerospace Medicine, Brooks Airforce Base, Texas, has done a thorough search for the sources you asked for. I regret to inform you that no sources have been found that link the lack of oxygen, anoxia, to hallucinations."

The core of David Ingvar's criticism was invalid. I answered his criticism in an article in *Sydsvenska Dagbladet* 8th of September 1981.

At The Hour Of Death was published after I had started work at the University of Iceland. All the royalties that I received I gave to a fund, which I used to pay expenses of further research I was conducting.

No other book had been published on deathbed visions until 2008 when Dr. Peter Fenwick at the

Institute of Psychiatry in London, co-authored with his wife, Elizabeth, *The Art of Dying: A Journey to Elsewhere*. They interviewed some forty nursing staff in hospices, who often witnessed patients having visions near the time of death. The nursing staff believed that the end-of-life-experiences (ELEs they called them) were a prognostic indicator for a nearing death. The Fenwicks concluded: "The carers we talked to in all our studies felt confident that ELEs are not drug induced" (Fenwick and Fenwick, 2008 p. 19).

This supports the findings of our study that is more thorough than any other published.

I have given many lectures on this subject in various countries. After the lectures, many people come up to me and tell me that they have been witness to such visions of family or friends. Interest in end-of-life-experiences is considerable and I am often asked to give lectures on the subject. I consider myself lucky to have had the opportunity to work with Karlis in those early days. It was uplifting for me and increased my interest in starting new projects.

I did not know Karlis well when we started working together. Later, someone said that we were very much alike: made from the same cloth, as he called it. Osis was a farmer's son from Latvia and came from Riga. When the Soviet rule was finally over in Latvia, Karlis received a letter from the authorities stating that he posessed a farm that had been lost to him while communists ruled the country. His brother had lived there until the end of World War II when the Russians captured the country. He was arrested and was never heard of again. Karlis Osis asked who was living on the land of his fathers and how that family fared. He was so generous as to give them the land. That described him well.

He was not fortunate enough to see the land of his youth again.

Osis had been working in the garden by his house in Glen Ridge, New Jersey where he lived with his wife, when he fell, broke his hip and was sent to the hospital. He died there a few days later on his eightieth birthday, 26th of December 1997. I wrote an obituary of my friend and colleague, which appeared in The *Journal of the Society for Psychical Research.*

8

OF THIS WORLD AND ANOTHER IN ICELAND

~

It had always been my intention to return to Iceland. A lecturer position in psychology was advertised at the University of Iceland. I applied, was hired, and should have started by the middle of 1973. I asked for six months leave to complete my work in New York.

Immediately I started to prepare a major survey of experiences and attitudes towards various psychic phenomena, religious experiences and folklore-related experiences. Much had been written about the experience of psychic phenomena, but an overview was lacking of how widespread they were in the modern day population. I heard that one of my friends in America, John Palmer, was thinking on the same lines and I adjusted my questionnaires to his for an easier comparison. He did his survey in the university town, Charlottesville in Virginia.

The town is not a realistic cross section of Americans. Those who answered were, on one hand, university students and, on the other hand, townspeople, most of whom worked either at the university or in jobs related to it; but the economic reality of the town rested on the activities of the university. The Icelandic questionnaire was longer than the American one as there were questions on Icelandic folklore-related belief and experiences as well as the questions that we had in common.

It was clear that funds, which I received from the university, would not be sufficient for such a major project. Nevertheless, I started with full force. I told a good old friend, Bjorn Franzson, about my concern. He had studied mathemathics and physics in Germany and had written a book in Icelandic on the physical world. A little later he contacted me. A businessman friend of his was ready to come up with the funds to conduct the survey: one more stroke of good luck.

This made it possible to buy an 1100 strong random national sample of the adult population from the Office of National Statistics (Hagstofa Islands), print questionnaires, mail them, etc. I received a printout of the sample of 1132 individuals in December 1974.

Few regulations existed on privacy protection at that time. Those who did not send back a completed questionnaire, we were able to contact again. Thus, in the end, 902 persons sent us completed questionnaires: a truly excellent response rate. The results were ready in 1975. I organized a meeting with the media and told them about the results, which were widely reported and even reached some foreign newspapers.

What caused most attention was that 64% of the sample reported some psychic experience: 57% of the men and 70% of the women. The most common were precognitive dreams, reported by 36%. It took me by surprise how common it was that people were aware of someone who had passed away: 31%. Immediately I felt that we had to investigate this further. That survey is reported in a later chapter. Experiences of poltergeist phenomena were reported by 18%.

Somewhat unexpected was how religious we Icelanders are. 15% were very religious and 63% quite religious. Only 3% were not religious at all. In this we were more like the Americans and less like the Scandinavian nations. Furthermore, the results showed that only 8% often read the Bible, but a lot more read books on psychic phenomena.

I rather expected that the majority believed in life after death, but was surprised how common belief in the afterlife was: 40% were certain of the afterlife; 28% considered it likely. Only 2% rejected it completely; for 5% it was unlikely, and possible for 20%.

After a thorough analysis of the data, I authored a book on the subject, *Thessa heims og annars* (*Of This World and Another*) which was published in Icelandic in 1978.

Not everybody was pleased with the attention, which the survey received, and I had a feeling that some people didn't like the results. A few foreign journalists wrote articles on how uniquely superstitious the Icelanders are. I have pointed out to those who came to interview me that no such extensive surveys have been conducted in their country, so how can they know the difference between Icelanders and other nations?

Psychic experiences have been surveyed elsewere, but with very few questions, apart from the survey in Charlottesville, but even that survey was not as comprehensive as ours.

Andrew Greeley, a sociologist, fiction writer and Catholic priest, had a few questions embedded in a large survey conducted by the National Opinion Research Center in Chicago:

Have you ever:

a. Felt as though you were in touch with someone when they were far away (extrasensory perception).

b. Seen events that happened at a great distance as they were happening (clairvoyance).

c. Felt that you were in touch with someone who had died (contact with the dead).

Greeley's questions were included in a survey, in the early eighties, that was conducted in most Western Europen countries. The U.S. and Italy were the most psychic nations with 60% reporting some psychic experience. Icelanders were in third place with 52%. Strange as it may seem, the Norwegians, whom we consider to be our closest relatives, were at the bottom of the list with 24% and the Danes with 25%. It was remarkable how much we differed from our neighbouring countries. We were much closer to the Italians and the Americans. It is difficult to find any adequate explanations for this result.

More Icelanders had "felt really in touch with someone who has died" than any other nation in Western Europe: 41%. Next came Italians with 34%. The average for Western Europe was 25%. Norway and Denmark were lowest with 9% and 10%. This survey was conducted twice in the U. S. several years apart. The figures were 30 and 41%; about the same as in Iceland.

Specific Icelandic Folk-Beliefs and Experiences

To some extent, every culture has its own way of conceptualizing psychic experiences, giving rise to location-specific beliefs and experiences. There are at least three kinds in Iceland, all related to our folklore.

Fylgja is the most common. Literally it means a "follower" and it's sometimes translated into English as "fetch, supernatural follower." It is related to the Norwegian *vardoger*. This is an ancient belief in the Nordic countries, perhaps also related to the more southern notion of a *daimon* or guardian angel that everybody is believed to have. For example, a knock is heard on the door but nobody is there when the door is opened. However, a few minutes later someone does arrive. This phenomenon is explained in terms of the visitor's *fylgja* having arrived ahead of them. Some persons have a greater reputation than others of having a *fylgja*.

There is a more macabre explanation of the origin of *fylgja*. In earlier centuries when there were no institutions in Iceland to take care of the desolate and homeless, the law required that every farm should shelter and feed such a person for three days and nights, if he or she knocked on their door. If a farmer rejected such a person, who then died on the way to the next farm, it was believed that the dead person might follow the farmer's family, and their descendants for several generations.

There is more belief in the *fylgja* phenomenon (spirit guardians) than in any other in Iceland, with 28% of respondents considering it certain or likely, 42% possible, and only 22% rejecting it as impossible or unlikely. One person in six reported having had such an experience in 1974 as well as in 2006.

Spell-spots (*álagablettir*) require an explanation. Elves are believed to dwell there or use them for magical purposes in some way; they are usually rocks or even a small piece of grassland. The elves are believed to have cast a spell on such spots so that if they are interfered with by humans (e.g. demolished or the grass cut) then the elves may exact revenge through a calamity befalling the person responsible, such as a serious sickness, accident or loss of fortune. Belief in spell-spots is thought to stem from Celtic countries. Roughly equal numbers of respondents accept and reject this belief, with 38% considering it possible, and hence not ruling it out. Personal experience of this is rare: only 3% in 2006 and 2% in 1974. This belief still exists in the western part of Ireland.

The last and best known is the belief in elves (*álfar*). More respondents reject that belief than accept it, but about a third of the respondents consider it possible that they may exist. Personal experience is quite rare: 5% in 2006 and in 1974. Icelandic folklore sometimes distinguishes between *álfar* (elves) and 'hidden people' (*huldufólk*), the latter being an invisible, parallel race, which lives much like ordinary humans. The *álfar*/elves are like the elves of Continental Europe: beings of light who are similar to the angels of Christianity. In our survey, 54% of respondents did not distinguish between elves and hidden people, but 20% did and 26% said they were not sure.

To illustrate what an elf may be, here is a case from the biography of a well-known labor leader, Tryggvi Emilsson, who was brought up on a sheep farm.

One day in his early youth he found himself far away from the farm, when he noticed a lamb that had become stuck on a small ledge on a cliff and unable to move up or down. The boy succeeded in climbing down from the top of the cliff to the lamb, but then discovered that he was unable to get back up to the larger ledge from which he had climbed down. As he brooded on his desperate situation he was called by his name. He looked up and saw a young girl with particularly beautiful eyes on the ledge above. She stretched her hand down, first for the lamb and then for him. As he got up to the ledge he turned round to thank the girl who had saved his life, but she had disappeared and was nowhere to be seen. The memory of her beautiful shining eyes and appearance remained with him as one of the most beautiful experiences of his life.

Perhaps others might have interpreted this experience differently, but, for him, she was an elf.

We have no comparable data on elves from other countries, although such beliefs and experiences are found in the Western part of Ireland. Because of the similarity of elves to angels, it may be that elves are a pre-Christian conception of angels. It may, therefore, be interesting to look at data on belief in angels in Europe. The 1999 wave of the European Values Survey included a question on belief in angels. The mean for the eight participating countries was 50%, with figures varying from 70% in Italy and Hungary to 24% in Germany. Iceland was slightly below the mean with 48% expressing belief in angels.

Terry Gunnell, associate professor of folklore at the University of Iceland, was interested in my 1974-75 survey and wanted us to repeat it. We constructed a new questionnaire consisting mostly of questions from 1974-75, deleted some and added a few. The survey was conducted in 2006 and 2007. The results were comparable for the most part. Not much had changed during a third of a century.

9

FACE TO FACE WITH SATHYA SAI BABA: "THE MAN OF MIRACLES"

⌢‿⌣

The first I heard of Sai Baba was when Karlis Osis and I were in Northern India. We sometimes asked those whom we met often, staff at hospitals or universities, whether they knew of any gurus, yogis or swamis who were gifted with psychic abilities or had demonstrated unusual control over their bodily functions. Usually the answer was no, but the name Sai Baba was more often mentioned than any other. We became curious. Later we met men who had come to know Sai Baba personally and that increased our interest. At this time his name was starting to spread through India, although he had not yet become known throughout the country. Outside of India, few knew of Sai Baba, but that was to change.

Among those things we heard about Sai Baba were incidents that were very strange, to say the least. It was said that he made objects appear and disappear, which he gave as gifts; these included jewellery, sweets and even fruit that wasn't in season, but, more often than not, he produced *Vibuti*, the ash from burnt cowdung, in large amounts, seemingly from nowhere. In India, *Vibuti* is equivalent to the sacramental wine and bread in Christianity. Cows are sacred in India and Indians have great reverence for them. Similarly, in Norse mythology we have Audhumla, the primeval cow.

We were told that *Vibuti* sometimes appeared on pictures of Sai Baba, even in distant parts of the country, and that he could read people's innermost thoughts, appear in dreams and then tell people about the dream, and that he even raised people from death. It is not uncommon in India to exaggerate and we asked ourselves if this was all exaggeration or if there was a grain of truth in these stories.

In December 1973, at the end of our third trip to India, Karlis and I decided to go to Puttaparti, Sai Baba's birthplace where he still lived. India is an extremely large country and we were in Northern India, whereas the village of Puttaparti is in the south of the country in the middle of the plateau. It was three hours flight from Delhi to Bangalore and, from there, three to four hours drive to Puttaparti. When we reached Prashanti Nilayam, his ashram in Puttaparti, several hundred people were there and everybody wanted to meet Sai Baba. We quickly arranged to have a meeting with him.

Sai Baba was well over forty when we met him. He was born on November 23, 1926. He reminded me more of Napoleon than a spiritual leader. Nevertheless, he was a charming man and he had a peculiar way of getting people under his influence and surprising them. Wherever he appeared he was the center of attention.

Baba always dressed in a simple saffron yellow tunic, without pockets, that fell to his ankles. He came out of his house twice a day, in the early evening and in the morning, and a multitude of people would be waiting on the sandy ground in front of his house which was called the Mandir. Everybody sat quietly, women on one side and men on the other. The guards, who were volunteers, were dressed in white with a red scarf around their neck. They saw to it that law and order was kept, but people were always trying to get to the front, particularly if they had been waiting for a long time. Some arrived early in the morning to get a good seat in the hope that that Baba would talk to them, or so they could give him a message or a request, which many often did. We assumed that people were mainly asking for favours of some kind, about their health, for instance, or asking for an interview, which was difficult to get because the multitude was huge.

After appearing from his house he would walk along the front row of the crowd, sometimes close to it, sometimes not so close, because some wanted to touch his feet or his garment and he did not seem to like that. One guard always walked closely behind him for safety. Baba would say a few words to some and accept letters from many. He would point to individuals and, sometimes, to small groups and they would be instructed to walk onto a platform at the house. These were the people to whom he would grant interviews.

After he had walked past the men and the women's side, he would walk swiftly to the house where a group awaited him, sitting on the concrete pavement. Then he invited a few into a small interview room, while others waited their turn.

Around lunchtime, singing and playing of instruments started in a hall in the building. This was the routine day after day. There was no weekend rest for Sai Baba.

Sometimes he left for Whitefield, which was near Bangalore, where he had a residence and ran a college. When that happened, many of the people would leave Puttaparti and hurry to Whitefield. There a similar routine repeated itself. Sai Baba appeared twice daily, although not as regularly as in Puttaparti, and everybody hoped to meet the miracle man.

On our first morning in Puttaparti we were immediately invited to sit on the concrete pavement by the house and soon we were invited into the interview room. Sai Baba asked the others who sat on the pavement if anyone spoke English and could interpret for us. An older man presented himself and came in with us. As we went inside, Sai Baba waved his hand in a circle-like motion and produced *Vibuti* which he gave to us. Then we all sat on the floor.

Karlis and I told him we had heard of his miracles and, before we got any further, he waved his hand again and a big shining gold ring lay in the palm of his hand. He put it on Karlis's finger and said it was a present for him. It fit him perfectly. In the ring there was a large enameled stone with a picture of Sai Baba and small notches held it firmly in the frame. It was a beautiful gold ring.

Karlis stated his admiration of the ring and added that we were primarily interested in a scientific research on his unique talents under controlled conditions. We knew very well what magicians can do, and we had to rule that out. Then a long conversation on the value of scientific research followed. Baba did not belittle science, but he seemed to think that science could never explain miracles. He said he only used miracles for good for those who believed in him. He did not use them for show. These words were obviously directed to us.

We tried, with eagerness, to convince him about the value of our cause. He, on the other hand, wanted to discuss the spiritual and the importance of the pure and religious life that could lead people to greater understanding. The conversation went back and forth and I felt we weren't getting anywhere. Then he said that spiritual and daily life should be intertwined like a double *rudraksha*. We asked what *rudraksha* was. He could not explain it to us, nor did the interpreter, who usually did not say much because Baba spoke quite good English. Perhaps I was a bit irritated that we were not getting anywhere, so I asked him repeatedly what double *rudraksha* was. He tried to explain it again but it wasn't clear to us. Then he seemed to lose patience; he waved his hand and opened the palm of his hand in front of me. "This is it," he said. In his palm was an object: two stones from a fruit half grown together, each one being a little larger than a prune stone and with folds like the brain.

I took it and observed it carefully then handed it to Karlis who looked at it and gave it to the interpreter. The interpreter looked and handed it back to Sai Baba. Then Baba held his hand out to me and said: "This is a present to you." In my hand was the double *rudraksha* but now with shields of gold above and beneath it, held together by a thin gold chain. On top of the upper shield was a small golden cross and on it a red stone that looked like a ruby.

Sai Baba told me that I should not show it to anyone. For quite a while I didn't. Later, I had it examined by the jewelry testing service at the Ministry of Commerce in London. They told me that the gold in the ring was at least 22 carat and the stone was a real ruby. Botanists later told me that a double *rudraksha* is very rare, so rare that the Botanical Institute of India in Calcutta had never managed to own a good one. Many years later I learned that the Smithsonian Museum in Washington has such an ornament, which had been bought from a maharaja family in India. That *rudraksha* is in a beautiful gold frame and is quite unlike mine.

We asked Sai Baba how he did this. His answer was short and not really scientific: "We are all like matches, but the difference between me and you is that there is a fire on mine." We didn't get a further explanation. Sai Baba was not a man of science. He often talked in parables, but he phrased his answers in his own style.

Sometimes he became lighthearted and said something that made us all laugh. He was, without a doubt, the master of the encounter. Always he gave presents, often to many, and one time he gave all of us an exceptionally tasty Indian sweet from his hand.

To cut a long story short, we made no progress with Sai Baba this time, but he did not rule it out that we might later. How he "materialized" his "creations" was still not clear to us and eventually we had to say goodbye because we ran out of time.

About a year later, Karlis and I returned to Prasanthi Nilayam, Sai Baba's ashram in Puttaparti, this time with a lawyer from Los Angeles, Sidney Krystal, and his wife, Phyllis, two doctors and one engineer: a group that Sai Baba had chosen. Again we were invited in.With his usual hand movement, which was a sign that now something would appear, Sai Baba produced a long gold chain with many glittering gemstones and handed it to Phyllis Krystal. The couple had an important wedding anniversary that day.

We sat on the floor. Karlis was beside me. He wore the beautiful gold ring that Sai Baba had given him on our previous visit. I could see the ring clearly and noticed that the people sitting next to us were admiring it. When we had walked in, Sai Baba did not shake our hands or touch us in any way. Again, we tried to convince him of our hopes of observing his producing physical objects under controlled conditions. As before, he turned the discussion towards the spiritual life and its value. Thus it went back and forth. He seemed to be getting bored with our talk about scientific research. All of a sudden he said to Karlis: "Look at your ring." We all looked. The stone with Sai Baba's picture that had been firmly fastened within the frame had suddenly disappeared from the ring; the space for the stone was empty. Then he said in a jovial manner, "This is my experiment."

We had been told that things do not just appear from Sai Baba, but they disappear too and now we had experienced that. I had seen the ring a few moments before with the stone intact and Baba had not come near us. We had no explanation for what had just happened. Later Karlis described our experience to a famous magician in New York. He said he could do all that he had observed *if* he was well prepared, except for the disappearing of the stone; he had no explanation for that, either.

It was clear that we were not getting anywhere with this mysterious man. While in Puttaparti, we got to know various people who had many remarkable stories to tell, in fact, so remarkable that they sounded impossible, if these were not just tricks. And some of these were important, highly educated people who had nothing to gain from revealing these events. One was the former president of Bangalore University, V.K. Gokak, S. Bagvantam, a nuclear physicist and, at one time, a head of the Indian Institute of Science in Bangalore; the other, D. K. Banerjee from the same institute. They told us of many things they had witnessed, which they couldn't explain by normal means.

One magician in India, Dr. Eruk Fanibunda, who had even received a prize in Britain for his magical abilities, had, like others, tried to solve the riddle. Dr. Eruk went to Puttaparti, followed Sai Baba for a while, but gave up. This was not sleight of hand, he thought; something real was taking place. I visited Eruk at his home in Mumbai some years later. He verified this to me. He had had many more opportunities to observe Sai Baba and, in hindsight, had not changed his mind. This was not magic.

I felt I needed to improve my understanding of magic; by magic I mean trickery. One magician acquaintance of mine was Marcello Truzzi who was also a professor in sociology at the University of Eastern Michigan. He was one of the co-founders of the Committee for the Scientific Investigation of Claims of the Paranormal (CSICOP) where philosopher Martin Gardner was president and magician James Randi was held in high esteem. By now Truzzi had left the organization, because of differences in their methods of challenging scientific research on psychic phenomena.

Through Truzzi's recommendation, I was accepted as a member of the International Brotherhood of Magicians. I got an opportunity to attend a convention where magicians showed each other their latest work, competed in various fields of magic, and sold their magic tricks. A whole industry has been built around this in the U.S. It was quite informative to get into their inner circle, but it did not help me to explain Sai Baba's phenomenon. I knew, perhaps a bit better, how he could have used magic to call forth some of what we observed. Whether he did it that way, was another matter. Then there were the phenomena that seemed impossible to explain in any way.

With my parents, Haraldur Oskar Erlendsson and Anna
Elisabet Elinmundardottir.

I was born in this house which my father and brothers
built just outside Reykjavik.

My mother and father, working in the fish factory where they met.

My father (centre) preparing salt-fish which was Iceland's main export prior to World War II.

My first visit abroad
with two classmates.
We spent the
summer working in
Sweden.

With classmates at a hut on Fimmvörduhals between
the glaciers Eyjafjallajökull and Myrdalsjökull after
several hours of strenuous hiking.

With my first wife, Helga Helgadottir.

Men who influenced my thinking and view of life in my early teens and twenties; Gretar Fells, president of the Theosophical Society in Iceland, Martinus a Danish philosopher and "seer" and Paul Brunton who wrote several books on spirituality and the inward path.

Margret Hjalmtysdottir whom
I first met when sailing with
Gullfoss to Copenhagen.
Margret and I lived together for
32 years until she passed away.

Professor Hans Bender in
Freiburg.

Karlis Osis.

BLAÐAMANNASKÍRTEINI Nr 81
(PRESS CARD)
Gefið út af Blaðamannafélagi Íslands
(Issued by The Icelandic Press Association)

Nafn ERLENDUR
      HARALDSSON
Blað ALTHYDUBLADID
er félagi í Blaðamannafélagi Íslands
(is a member of The Icelandic Press
Association)

(P. t. form.)   (Eiginhandarundirskrift)

Íslands Journalistforbund medlem af International Federation of Journalists anbefaler   1961
ihændehaveren af dette kort til Deres be-
vågenhed og beder Dem yde ham al den
bistand og hjælp, som kan gavne ham per-
sonlig eller den avis, han arbejder for

The Icelandic Press Association member of
International Federation of Journalists re-   1962
commends the bearer of this card to your
kind favour and attention and begs you to
render him any assistance and support which
may be of value to him and the paper he
represents.

L'organisation de la Presse islandaise mem-
bre des Federation Internationale des Jour-   1963
nalistes demande que le porteur de cette carte
soit reçu avec bien veillance, et qu'on lui prête
de toute façon possible, l'aide et l'appui qui
seront utiles à lui et à son journal.

This press card opened many doors
during my time in Berlin.

With freedom-loving Kurds in Iraq. There we travelled
secretly, mostly at night by mule, donkeys or by hiking,
for fear of air attacks.

Kabul. Less veiled women and a touch of central Asia.
Afghanistan was ruled by a king at his time.

With Sai Baba at Puttaparthi

With Mulla Mustafa Barzani, leader of the freedom fighting Kurds. I wrote later a book in their struggle for autonomy that appeared in Icelandic and German.

In the woods with J. B. Rhine, his wife Louisa, my second
wife Helga and Ulrich Timm from Freiburg.

Ian Stevenson, professor of psychiatry at the University
of Virginia in Charlottesville.

With my second wife, Helga Haraldsson.

Karlis Osis and myself with assistants in India, who
worked with us on the research for the book
At the Hour of Death.

With coworkers in Sri Lanka, who researched children, who remembered a past life with me. That research resulted in the book *I Saw a Light and Came Here*.

With Purnima Ekanayake and my interpreter Ratnayake. Purnima remembered her life as an incense maker.

At Potala in Lhasa, Tibet.

With the prime minister of Iraqi Kurdistan, Barzani, the son of Barzani I walked through the mountains with.

As a young man in Copenhagen.

10

BILOCATION AND CHANGING
WATER INTO PETROL

~

The ASPR was unwilling to fund further research after our second visit to Sai Baba because no experiments were in sight. I decided to use my royalties from *At the Hour of Death* to continue. I planned to interview numerous people who had come to know Sai Baba, particularly those who had stayed with him over a long period, or had been his assistants and served him in some way.

There was a rather frequent turnover among those who were around him for a considerable time. Most of them were young, often students, or retired people. Neither group stayed for long. However, I traced a number of people who had been close to him at various times in his life. They had washed his clothes and knew better than anyone where his clothes and things were kept. They also knew about all his possessions. They all had the same story to tell: they had no idea how Sai

Baba produced all these objects. All were convinced that it would not have been possible for him to hide the things that he gave away in his robe or elsewere, without their noticing it.

I made an effort to contact some of those who criticized Sai Baba. I met Hosur Narasimhaiha, who had been the president of the University in Bangalore and had founded a committee to research Sai Baba. He started by informing the media about what he was going to do and by publishing the letter he sent Sai Baba. He received no reply. Interestingly, the committee received numerous letters from people who had become acquainted with Baba. Narasimhaiha told me that they had really scrutinized these letters, and had not found anything that could explain the phenomena.

Nobody seemed to have a clue about how he did what he did. Later, a long time after my inquiries, stories started to circulate from former students at Sai Baba's colleges that they had observed some ornaments with him before he gave them away. In the latter part of his life such stories were quite numerous. Whether they were anything more than rumors, I cannot say.

There were also rumors, some supported by testimony, that he had had sexual relationship with men. More damaging for Western devotees, were claims of sexual relationships with young boys.

Some people tried to explain his phenomena by saying that he hypnotized his audience. It is never possible to hypnotize all. Those who hypnotize on stage always start with a large group and do light exercises to single out those who are easily hypnotized. Hypnosis could obviously not explain Sai Baba's phenomena.

Many of those, who had known Sai Baba for a long time, told truly amazing stories about him. While he was younger and fewer people were around him, they would often walk to the Chitravati River and sit there on the sand. Sometimes he would pile up a heap of sand, put his hand into it, draw out a hot pancake and give to someone. When that person received the pancake not one grain of sand was on it. And it was hot, in fact so hot it was difficult to hold. At one time he made a pile of sand and pulled out a statue of Lord Krishna. On that occasion the university president Gokak had been present.

Probably, the oddest of all that happened, in his early days, was when he was walking with a group of people around him. Suddenly he disappeared and then was heard calling from nearby and seen there. I interviewed several people who had witnessed this "bilocation." The incidents when he made himself disappear occurred only when he was young. A few times he suddenly disappeared from among them, appearing instantly on a nearby hill with a blinding light shining around him. This resembles the Biblical accounts of the Transfiguration on the Mount.

The third group whom I made an effort to trace were those who had been close to Sai Baba, but had turned their backs on him for one reason or another, or Sai Baba had pushed them away. I reasoned that these men (and they usually were men) would be more likely to tell if they were aware of deceptions taking place. I found two and neither of them claimed any deception ever took place. They had left Sai Baba for other reasons.

I became acquainted with a member of a raja family. The maharajas were wealthy, but lost their power when India became independent after World War II. Gopal Krishna was the son of the Raja of Venkatagiri. He had come to know Sai Baba early in his life and introduced me to various people who had been with Baba when he was a young man. Being with Gopal and having my *rudraksha* ornament seemed to open all doors.

The story of how Gopal came to know Sai Baba is interesting. His father wanted to invite Sai Baba to his palace. The custom is to send someone from the family to fetch the person in question and the more important the guest, the closer to the Raja the person sent is. The Raja wanted to send his son Gopal to Baba and have him accompany him to the palace. Gopal refused to go because he had no interest in gurus or swamis.

Shortly after falling asleep that evening, Gopal dreamed that Sai Baba came and brought him a mango fruit; his favourite fruit. The fruit in the dream tasted delicious. That dream changed everything. He went to his father and said he was ready to go. He and his attendants set out in the middle of the night and arrived in Puttaparti around lunchtime. They came to the Chitravati River that runs by the village and there stood Sai Baba on the other side of the river. Before they could say anything, Sai Baba said to Gopal Krishna: "The mango made you run here." After that he was convinced that Sai Baba's miraculous powers were real.

With the assistance of Gopal Krishna, I got in touch with many who had known Sai Baba from earlier times. He also helped me to find two men who had turned their back on Baba. One of them was Varadu. He had made a habit of drinking and was a bit of a rake. Sai Baba had asked him to leave, accusing him wrongly of certain things. Varadu was angry with him for this; nevertheless, when I intereviwed him he told me that if he felt bad he still prayed to Sai Baba.Varadu had been witness to an endless stream of miracles and he did not doubt them. One time when they were down by the sand banks of the river, Sai Baba took some water out of the muddy river for him and it was completely pure and sweet tasting.

The other man who had turned his back on Sai Baba was Krishna who lived in Hyderabad. He had met Sai Baba early on and had become extremely close to him. I suspect they had a love relationship. Then they parted ways. Krishna went away, turned against him and became a Christian – a profound Christian.

Neither of these men thought that Sai Baba was some kind of god or avatar as it is called in Hinduism. However, they had no explanation of how he performed all the miracles. Krishna had been very close to him and told me that he had known all the depository boxes where Sai Baba kept his things and knew his living quarters well. He did not doubt that what Sai Baba was seen to do was real. Krishna found a fruit named kova very tasty. Sai Baba knew how much he loved kova and every time Krishna asked Sai Baba, he would make that fruit appear, be it summer or winter, the season for the fruit or not. Krishna and Varadu had a disappointing experience with Sai Baba and had their doubts about his religious ideas, particularly his claim of being an avatar (god-sent prophet). However, neither of them doubted that he had supernatural talents.

I went thirteen times to India in connection with Sai Baba, mostly between 1976 and 1983. I did not meet him on every visit, but a few times we met. I last saw him in 2005 when I was doing research in Sri Lanka. Great festivities were going on in a newly built crowded stadium. I saw him only from afar. He was in a wheelchair; he had broken his hip and, later, his hand.

Sai Baba's predictions about people did not always come to pass. I realized this after many interviews and a survey that I did among 30 people who had known him closely. He had been astoundingly smart to predict his own life at the beginning. As a teenager he told that an immense multitude of people would storm to Puttaparti, such a crowd that his old disciples would have to use binoculars to see him. It came to pass. On the other hand, he was 10 years off with the prediction of his own death. He said he would die in 2021, but he died in 2011.

Some claim that fragments from films show that he used tricks, but it is not certain whether these film fragments show it, but possible. No experiments exist, no certain knowledge about what was going on, but a great amount of eyewitness testimony.

Wealthy people poured money on Sai Baba. He used it to build schools and hospitals in various places in India. Isaac Tigrett the founder of the Hard Rock restaurant chain was one of them. He funded a large high-tech hospital built in Puttaparti, furnished with the newest technology. Sai Baba had a huge irrigation system built, so large that the government of India issued a stamp about it. It cost billions of Euros. Sai Baba greatly emphasized generosity and assistance to those who have not fared well in life. Once he said that generous hands were more favored by God than praying lips. Devotional and religious singing played a great role in his movement.

Sai Baba came from a family of poor farmers. At thirteen years of age he said that he was Sai Baba of Shirdi reborn. Sai Baba of Shirdi (1837-1918) was a holy man who lived in Shirdi, a small town not far from Mumbai, and he was influential in reconciling Muslims and Hindus.

The young Sai Baba started, at this time, to hand out sweets, flowers and ice cream. Apparently, it was as if he manifested them out of the air around him. Disciples started to gather around him; the crowds grew larger and larger and the first ashram was built.

People came from all over the country and beyond to see him. In one of many anacdotes it was claimed that at one time one could barely drive to Puttaparti and there was no local petrol station; Ranjoth Singh arrived in his luxury car and ran out of petrol and he had to get back to Bangalore. He told Sai Baba about his problem. Baba asked one of his assistants, Amarendra Kumar, to fetch a bucket and fill his tank with water. With his tank full, Ranjoth Singh drove to Bangalore. Four other witnesses told me about the same kind of incidences. Did they all lie? Were they all deceived? Or was this similar to when Jesus changed water to wine?

I once asked Sai Baba why he could do such astonishing things and we could not. He answered that he thought, imagined and then the thing came into existence. It was as simple as that.

There were more accounts that he had disappeared from one place and later appeared truly far away. One event had happened in the state Kerala on the south west coast of India. Karlis and I visited those involved and interviewed them. A young girl was ill and Sai Baba appeared at her home. With her family he performed a sacred ceremony where religious songs and hymns were sung and all participated in the singing. He told the family to invite the neighbors. The people thought Sai Baba had been visiting Kerala because, all of a sudden, he appeared in the doorway at this family's home. After the ceremony it became obvious that nobody had heard that he was in Kerala. In fact he had, at the same time, been visiting the palace of the raja of Venkatagiri, which is on the east coast and more than six hundred kilometres away. Karlis saw that he had signed the guestbook of the Venkatagiri family on the same day that he appeared in Kerala.

These stories of Sai Baba remind one of the stories of another man, Padre Pio, a monk who lived in Italy in the twentieth century (1887-1968) and whom the Catholic Church has now made a saint. Some of the stories of Padre Pio are similar to those of Sai Baba, but he did not create any objects. Among things said about him was that he appeared to people in different parts of the country.

As I wrote earlier, Sai Baba gave *Vibuti* more frequently to people than anything else. *Vibuti* also appeared often on pictures of him that people had placed in their home. I visited many such places, in India and also in other countries.

One example: I had planned a trip to Sri Lanka where I did research on children who claimed memories of a past life. I was late and I did not have the time to get a visa by mail from the embassy in Stockholm. I had to visit Lebanon, so I decided to apply for a visa in Beirut.

I filled out a form and handed it in with my passport. I was told I could wait. A while later, a secretary came and told me that the consul wanted to see me. The elderly man sat in his office, and flipped through my passport. He then said: "I feel I recognize the name. Are you not the one who wrote a book about Sai Baba?" I said: "yes." Then he said he had to tell me something. His grown up daughter had been seriously ill. In despair he prayed to Sai Baba because he had heard that it could help. The daughter recovered. He got a big picture of Sai Baba, framed with glass, and hung it in his bedroom. Soon *Vibuti* started to appear on the picture. He told me that he lives on an upper floor in the building and he could show this to me if I wanted. He brought me into his bedroom. Opposite the bed hung a large picture of Sai Baba. Distinct stripes of vibuti lay on the glass and also between the glass and the picture. Also a trace of *amrith* (thick liquid) often referred to by Indians as the eternal drink. It sometimes appears with *Vibuti* on pictures. Bear in mind we were in Beirut. The consul general had never been to Puttaparti; he had never met Sai Baba, and he kept this a family secret.

I finally wrote *Miracles Are My Visiting Cards*, a book about Sai Baba which was published in 1987. It has been published in many languages and in various parts of the world. Sai Baba died on the 24th of April 2011. I visited Puttaparti in 2013, made many inquiries, and wrote an extended and revised edition of my book but with a new title: *Modern Miracles: Sathya Sai Baba: The Story of a Modern Day Prophet.*

11

EXPERIMENTS ON HEALING
AND PRECOGNITION

~

My interest in conducting experiments continued after my memorable year with J. B. Rhine. In spite of involvement in surveys and studies of spontaneous cases such as deathbed visions, encounters with the departed and claims of past life memories, and investigating individual psychics like Hafsteinn Bjornsson and Sathya Sai Baba, I still found time for a few experiments. Two accounts follow.

Experiments On Healing

In 1972 I conducted the following experiment with Thorsteinn Thorsteinsson, a biochemist in the faculty of medicine at the University of Iceland. Can mental intention, prayer, or whatever we want to call it, have an effect on a living organism?

Seven subjects took part in the experiment: two spiritual healers and one dentist who was interested in spiritual healing. We shall refer to them as "healers." Four students who had no interest in healing also took part. We refer to these latter as "non-healers."

It can be quite complicated and cumbersome to test the effect of a treatment on patients. It was decided, therefore, to test the effect on a simple living system. Healers were asked to direct their healing to grow yeast. A small amount of yeast (0.25gr.) was put into a nutritive solution (water, glucose, NaCl, KaCl, NH4Cl, MgSO4, NaPO3), and shaken until homogeneous. This solution was poured into twenty test tubes, each containing 10 ml. The test tubes were randomly divided into two groups of ten; experimental and control. They were sealed and simultaneously placed in front of a subject who was instructed to try for ten minutes, by a mental method of his or her choice, to increase the growth of the yeast in the solution. The subject was not allowed to touch the test tubes, or to come within a foot of them. Then all the test tubes were stored in the same place for 24 hours, after which the growth of the yeast was measured by a light-absorbance calorimeter.

A research assistant, who was not aware of which tubes were experimental and which control, conducted the measuring process and, as a backup, they were also measured by one of the experimenters. Thus, there were two measurements of yeast growth for each test tube and the mean of these measurements was used to calculate the effect.

Seven subjects participated in a total of twelve sessions. Five subjects had two sessions, and two had one. Each session was conducted as described above, so that there was a total of 240 test tubes used in the experiment: 120 for treatment and 120 for control. For purposes of analysis, each experimental tube was paired with a control tube used in the same session, and the growth of the yeast in the two tubes was compared.

The results indicated that mental concentration/intention/prayer/spiritual healing affected the growth of the yeast. In the 120 pairs of test tubes there was more growth in 58 of the experimental tubes than in the corresponding control tubes; in 33 there was less growth; and in 29 pairs the growth was equal in experimental and control tubes.

The important finding in this experiment is the fact that the bulk of the positive scoring was done by the three "healers" ($z = 3.80$; $P = .00014$, two tailed), whereas the "non-healers" (students) gave chance results ($z = .08$).

We can infer from this experiment that positive mental intention can have a beneficial effect on the health of patients: not only on patients, but perhaps also on ourselves. It may show the importance of cultivating our garden of thought, namely to have a positive approach to life and avoid negative thinking. Our way of thinking may influence our health more than we are aware of.

The Effect Of Belief On Precognition

Is it possible for us to have an inkling of what lies ahead of us? Can we predict things/events without having any rational reasons to guide us? Are we more likely to be able to do so, if we believe that this is possible in principle?

We tested the hypothesis that performance in a precognition test (guessing game) is related to the belief in the existence of psychic phenomena and/or taking an interest in the subject, for instance, reading about it. We asked 449 students – from 25 classes in vocational schools, high schools and colleges – these two questions and gave them a test of precognition:

1. Do you think that the existence of telepathy and precognition is: a) unthinkable, b) possible and 3) certain?
2. Do you read books or articles on psychic matters: a) often b) seldom, c) never?

The experiment was planned by me and carried out by eleven students of psychology I supervised. Apart from answering these two questions, every participant was asked to guess which of five different letters, L, X, Y, O, Z, the university computer would randomly select for each of a hundred numbered cells, which were printed on a sheet of paper that was given to each participant. It was stated that the computer would select the hundred random letters separately for each participant.

After all of the participants had filled in their hundred guesses, they were numbered from 1 to 449 in alphabetical order for each class; classes of each experimenter were numbered according to the median age of the class; and, finally, experimenters were put in alphabetical order with all of their participants. Thus, participant number 1 was the student whose name was first in alphabetical order in the youngest class of the experimenter who was first in the alphabetical order of the eleven experimenters.

When all subjects had been numbered, we obtained 449 sets of 100 random letters from the university computer. For each participant, the set of random letters that carried his number was compared with what letter the participant had written in the 100 cells of his sheet. It was counted as one hit each time a participant had written into a cell the same letter as the computer had selected for that cell. The number of hits that each subject made served as a measure of his precognition. All steps in the evaluation were carried out three times to avoid possible errors.

By chance alone we can expect to get 20 hits on average for each participant, since five different letters were used and each subject made 100 trials. The mean number of hits for all 449 subjects was 19.86, which doesn't deviate significantly from the theoretical mean.

However, when we divide the participants according to the way they answered our questions, we find significant differences in their performance.

Belief in telepathy or precognition

Of our 449 subjects, 90 thought that the existence of telepathy and precognition was certain. They made 41 more correct guesses than they should have by pure chance, and thus obtained a mean of 20.46. The 331 who thought that these phenomena could possibly exist obtained 55 fewer hits than they should have by pure chance, with a mean of 19.83 hits. The 28 who thought the existence of ESP was unthinkable obtained 49 fewer hits than they should have obtained by pure chance, with a mean of 18.25. This deviation is significantly below chance (z -2.32).

A chi-square test that takes into account the ranks of the three groups reveals a significant relationship between the number of correct guesses and belief in the existence of ESP (x^2=5.59, 1df, p=.02). This is a confirmation of the so-called sheep-goat effect, which is the effect whereby believers in psychic abilities score better than non-believers. It is usually found only with a relatively large number of subjects. Expressed in percentages, the deviations from the theoretical means are nearly always very small, the sheep (believers) scoring slightly above chance and the goats (disbelievers) scoring slightly below, as in the present experiment.

Reading of psychical material

Of our 449 subjects, 105 often read articles or books about psychical phenomena. They had 92 correct guesses above chance and obtained a mean score of 20.88 hits (z=+2.01, P=.04, one tailed).

The 225 participants who seldom read articles or books about psychical phenomena obtained 23 hits below chance. That gives a mean score of 19.91, which is very close to the theoretical mean of 20.00.

The 89 participants who never read about psychical phenomena obtained 132 fewer correct guesses than they should have by pure chance. Their mean for correct guesses was 18.52, substantially below the theoretical mean of 20.00. Their result was highly significant (z=-3.50, P=.0005, one-tailed).

The main purpose of the experiment was to test if the frequency of reading psychical material affects the capacity for precognition. It does. The results reveal a highly significant relationship between the number of correct guesses and the frequency of reading of psychical material. There was a highly significant difference between the three groups (x^2=16.62, 1 df, p=.00005).

Females have a reputation of being more "intuitive" than males. Perhaps that was expressed by the fact that women had more deviant mean scores than men in the results regarding belief in telepathy and precognition. The means for the females were 20.74, 19.99 and 17.23, whereas they were 20.19, 19.61 and 19.13 for males.

For the reading of books and articles on psychic matters, the figures were 21.07, 19.91 and 18.29 for females and 20.44, 19.91 and 18.72 for males.

12

THE DEPARTED
AMONG THE LIVING

~

"Have you ever perceived or felt the nearness of a deceased person?" 31% of the large sample of our 1974-75 survey responded with a yes: 36% of the women and 24% of the men. This unexpected finding opened up many questions. What was the nature of this experience? How were the departed perceived? Who were they? Under what circumstances did the experience take place?

We sent a brief questionnaire to subscribers of a few journals and asked if they, in a waking state, had experience of people who had died. Fishermen and people in the fishing industry, farmers and those interested in spiritual and psychic phenomena, primarily read these journals. The subscribers were around nine thousand. We received about 700 questionnaires with positive responses. Some did not meet our criteria, such as dreams and experiences with mediums, and were excluded. If they had more than one experience of the departed, they were asked to report the most impressive experience.

In-depth interviews were conducted in the early 1980s over the telephone and tape-recorded. We began by asking each respondent to give a detailed description of his or her most memorable experience, and then we went through all the relevant questions in a long questionnaire that we had developed. Our plan was to get an approximately equal number of cases from men and women.

The alleged encounters came in a great variety of forms. Ninety percent were sensory: visual, auditory, tactile, olfactory, or a combination of these. Ten percent consisted only of a vivid sense of presence.

Visual apparitions dominated and were 69% of the cases. The content varied widely. Three examples follow:

1. This happened three years ago. I sat in a chair in my room and was reading. Then I looked up and saw my deceased grandmother standing in front of me, as fully alive. I told my mother about this the following day. She said, "That is nice, it was her birthday." I had not remembered it.

2. I had recently started working in a factory when one day I saw a man walking at the other end of the machine at which I was working. He walked up to a wall near which the machine was placed and back. I went to see who the man was but found no one. When I told my co-workers about this experience and described the man to

them; they were sure that this was a ghost, which some others had also seen. He was the former director of the company who had committed suicide.

3. I brought my wife to the hospital in February 1960. She had been sick for several weeks. I visited her that same evening again and she was dressed in a blue nightgown. I had expected to see her again the following day but she died in the night. The next day my daughter-in-law came to select a gown for her burial. A day later I came home late and took out the psalm book to select the psalms to be sung at her funeral. Then the astounding thing happened. My wife suddenly stood in front of me, bathed in white light of an oval form. I saw her very distinctly and vividly as she held both hands around the collar of her nightgown: not that one I saw her in when I saw her the last time, but a pink fancy gown she used only rarely. She held the collar together with both her hands under her cheek. I became startled and then she disappeared. I had not known what gown my daughter-in-law had selected for her but discovered later that it was exactly this dress.

The apparition was seen through open eyes in 89% of the visual cases. In 7% the percipient saw the deceased person as if by the mind's eye, as a vivid image in the mind. In a few other cases (4%), the respondent was not sure if the apparition was perceived internally or externally, as in the following:

> As a young girl I rented a room here in Reykjavík. It had been a storage room for firewood and no one had lived in it before me. I am not psychic, but bit-by-bit I began to realize there was a person in the room; someone friendly and it was a man. As winter came I could detect what he looked like; slowly it became clear to me. It did not happen suddenly. ... The man was pleasant and I felt he was always asking me to pray for him. Then one rather cold evening, I had turned the lights off and faced the wall ready to go to sleep. Sometimes I would cover myself with two blankets, but now I distinctly felt that I was being covered, just like a mother covers a child. It was the man tending to me, but at the same time he constantly asked me to pray for him. I didn't hear any words; it was rather like a message was being pressed into me; that is how I sensed it.
>
> I neither heard nor saw anything. I sensed it like this ... I don't know how to describe it. I understood the message although it was not put in words. Once when [I was] paying the rent the landlord asked jokingly if I had ever noticed anything in the room. There was a silence, so his wife scolding said to him that one should not ask questions like that. I thought it best to tell it like it was and let them have a laugh on me and said, "Why yes, there is a man in my room, a young man, but he isn't unfriendly."

The landlord seemed startled and said, "Why do you say that?"

"Well I'm not quite sure ... but he is friendly; he looks after me more than anything; there is no hostility between us."

The landlord asked if I could describe this man and so I did. He was rather distinct, had curly hair and unusual characteristics. Although they were not outstanding he was easy to describe. The landlord was very surprised, and looked stunned. He asked if I knew what had happened in the room. I said I had no such knowledge, but asked if the room had not been used for storage of firewood.

The landlord answered, "Yes it was, but a man committed suicide in that room a long time ago and your description fits him perfectly ... ." My description was in accordance with what the landlord had been told about the man, when he bought the house. I wasn't upset by all of this. I felt he was friendly, pleasant and pleading, and that he was grateful that I had prayed for him.

Auditory cases were the second most common: 28% of the experiences were auditory and 66% of these were of human voices. Voices alone without some other modality were rare. Two such cases were reported by fishermen and were warnings of impending danger:

1. This happened when I was a teenager. I was alone fishing on a small boat. Suddenly I

heard a voice that said I should leave the fishing line and row ashore. I heard this quite clearly. It was said in a commanding tone. I did as ordered. I do not know why, but I found it so odd. Just as I was about to arrive at the harbor, suddenly there swept over a violent storm. I barely managed to dock. I did not recognize the voice, but, later, I connected it with my brother who had recently drowned.

2. I was on a fishing boat from Stykkisholmur. We were out in the bay, in the storm and rain, and had just laid our nets and should be awakened at six the following morning. I slept in the narrow cabin with the others and one man was on duty in the deckhouse. At about five in the morning I and some others woke up as someone called "rise." I went up to the cabin door and called to the man in the deckhouse and asked if he had been calling. No, he said, it was not time for that. I went back to my bunk, and was not yet asleep, when again there was a shout, "Rise, are you not going to get out of bed?" It was as if someone was calling loudly from the cabin door some two meters away. Everyone woke up and jumped out of bed. That surprised me; generally the crew was not that quick. I told the machinist to run after and start the donkey engine to haul in the nets. As the machinist went down to the engine room he saw the dynamo catching fire.

He barely managed to disconnect from the electricity so that it came to a halt. I am convinced that if he had gone later we would have caught fire and there would have been a fatal explosion in the engine room. I did not recognize the voice. It called in a typical seaman fashion. I had reasons to suspect that it was my deceased grandfather.

Fairly common (30%) among the auditory cases were noises from various human activities that had been typical for a particular deceased person.

Shortly after our father died I came to his house with my brother. We knew that there was nobody in the house and then we heard the old man at his desk. He was walking around, opened the door and closed it again. Both of us stopped and listened when we entered and then I remarked, "I guess there is no doubt who is up there." "No there is no doubt about it," my brother replied. Both of us went upstairs; no one was there. We had heard this so clearly. He was 85 years old when he died, walked slowly you know; he had the typical old man's way of walking.

We contacted the respondent's brother, who said he remembered clearly that this event had taken place, but he could give no details. When we read the above account to him, he said it all came back to him, and he confirmed everything in his brother's account.

Thirteen percent of the cases were tactile, involving a touch sensation. Three quarters of these tactile cases involve two or more modalities. Here is one involving only the sense of touch:

> My mother and my father-in-law died only a few months apart and I sensed one of them. I think it was my mother. I sat at a table and was working when I felt someone come up behind me, bend down and tightly grab my shoulder. At first I naturally thought it was someone in the household. I looked back but did not see anyone. Then I realized what it was ... it was a cold and tight grip, and it was not from anyone in the household. In a strange way I was astounded; I sort of jumped up when I realized what it was, and I thought this would intimidate the person who was trying to comfort me, someone who was trying to get close to me because I was probably a little depressed. I felt as if someone had come to comfort me. ... I never had an experience like this again.

This following case combines vision, hearing, and touch:

> The night after my husband died I could not sleep, was at home in my bed and very lonely. Suddenly I sensed him standing by my bed. He seemed to be covered in something like mist. I saw him and felt his hand as he stroked my head and he recited a part of a well-known poem that was about how good it was to rest and then wake up one day surrounded by eternal joy. I felt quite differently after this.

The olfactory cases were the fewest: only 4% of the total number of cases. Some olfactory cases have very interesting features, although they have generally not been given much attention in the literature. Here are three olfactory cases:

1. I lived in Sandgerdi where we had just bought a house two months ago. I was alone in the house. My husband was out working. Suddenly I saw that a man entered through the front door and went to the kitchen. This happened suddenly and was over. I then felt a strong smell of liquor. I never use alcohol. Well, then my husband came home, and he said, "Who has been here?"
"Nobody," I tell him.
"Oh, there is such a strong smell of liquor."
"Yes," I say, "but nobody has been here ..."
The next day my husband came home for supper and said, "No wonder there was a liquor smell here yesterday ... Erlingur from whom we bought the house was missing in Siglufjordur yesterday ...." He had been quite drunk and it was feared that he had fallen into the harbor and drowned. Two weeks later his body was found floating in the harbor. When this incident occurred, we had no idea about what had happened. My husband is now deceased.

2. I was getting out of bed and then smelled a particular perfume that my wife always used. She had died some time back and this

smell had no normal cause or explanation that I was aware of. My wife was making me aware of her to comfort me.

3. My niece died from lung cancer. Most people with serious lung or digestion diseases have a bad odor, the smell of something rotting. One Sunday morning, some time after she passed away, I smelt this stink very clearly in the kitchen where I was working. I looked around to see if something in the kitchen could cause this but found nothing. Not an hour had passed when her husband came unexpectedly to visit. I considered this clearly to be her odor. I was not thinking about her, because some time had passed since her death. I do not remember the date, but I presume it was close to a year between these events. I felt it was exactly the smell she had after she became very ill ... I only first thought of her when her husband arrived.

About 10% of the experiencers reported a case that consisted solely of a vivid sense of presence and hence does not technically fall under the category of apparitions. They were included because our purpose was not only to study apparitions but also to uncover what kinds of experiences tend to be interpreted as encounters with the dead. Three such cases follow:

1. I have had this kind of experience a few times. One of them is especially memorable. My eye had been bothering

me for quite some time. I had something in my eye and I was quite uncomfortable. Then one morning, I was awake with my eyes closed when I felt my mother, who was deceased, standing at my bed. She bent over me and I thought I could feel her breathing. I was wide awake but did not want to open my eyes because I felt sure I would not see her. I am sure she was there and was checking how my eye was. I felt her bend down all the way to my face.

2. I had just woken up. A deceased woman, whom I knew very well, came to me and took me in her arms. This perception only lasted a few moments. When I was talking about this that same morning, my daughter said, "I also dreamt about her last night."

3. I was out in the country and going to visit my grandfather. I was having a pleasant trip, stayed at Blanda for two nights, or rather, was going to. I was not in any hurry. All of a sudden I sensed my grandfather right there with me. I instantly knew that he had passed away, went to the post office and called. It was confirmed that he had died the day before.

It is evident that some of the cases in this section involve more than one modality; in fact, 22% of them do: visual and auditory (10%); visual, auditory, and tactile (6%); visual and tactile (4%); and auditory and tactile (2%).

Our collection of cases does not confirm the popular belief that apparitions are mostly seen in darkness or twilight. Half of the experiences (52%) occurred either in daylight or full electric light, 33% in twilight, 10% in darkness, and some 4% under variable conditions.

In half of our cases the experiencer was working or actively engaged in some way, which gives some support to the reports above. An additional 22% were resting. Still, a sizable number of the encounters (28%) occurred just prior to falling asleep or upon awakening, many of them quite impressive. The following case happened immediately upon awakening to a man working on a fishing vessel.

> This happened during the summer of 1966. I was somewhere between sleeping and waking, when I became wide awake. I saw a man at the stove of the cabin; a young man who was stooping over it. He was doing something there. I recognized that this man was not a member of the crew. I was going to check this further, but then he disappeared. Later I got the information that he had got burnt inside the cabin. He did not get burnt to death: he suffocated in smoke. I remember so clearly that he was wearing a blue sweater and a scarf around his neck. My description fit what I later learnt about him.

Who were the departed that our experiencers had encountered? Read more about that in the next chapter.

13

WHO WERE THOSE ENCOUNTERED?

~

Unexpectedly, in my study the apparitions were predominantly male (67%). This surprising dominance of males is remarkably uniform in the experiences of both male and female experiencers. This has been found in analysis of the cases in *Phantasms of the Living* (1922), which involved death; 63% of the apparitions were male and 37% female. Very similar figures are found for both male and female percipients. Why were men more prevalent?

This predominance of males is also reflected in the kinds of relatives that are predominantly encountered. For example, 43 percipients encountered their father, whereas only 22 encountered their mother; 21 perceived their grandfather and 16 their grandmother; 18 widows perceived their deceased husband, whereas only 9 widowers perceived their deceased wife.

Rather frequent were encounters with a person who had committed suicide:

Jakob was a patient in a sanatorium where I worked. He was sometimes depressed, and I tried to brighten his stay with a bit of humor. One day I had talked to Jakob that he should visit us because he came from the same county as my husband and they would enjoy talking about the people from there. He says yes to that, he is glad, and I say to him: "You promise to come tomorrow."

"Yes, yes, I promise," he says. During the night, I wake up, and all strength is like taken away from me. I am unable to move. Suddenly I see the bedroom door opened and on the threshold stands Jakob, with his face all covered with blood. I look at this for a good while, unable to speak or move. Then he disappeared and I felt as if he closed the door behind him. I became my normal self, called my husband and told him about the incident: "I can swear that something has happened at the sanatorium." I telephoned in the morning and asked if everything was all right with Jakob. "No," said the nurse, "he committed suicide last night."

We interviewed the husband. He told us that his wife had awakened him in the middle of the night and told him about what she had seen. They did not know Jacob's fate until the following morning. Further inquiries revealed that on the morning of October 8, 1962, Jakob was missing from his room. The police were called and a few hours later he was found drowned some hundred yards downstream from a pedestrian bridge over a river close to the sanatorium. The post-mortem report declared the cause of death as "suicidum submergio," that is, suicide by drowning. In the report, it was written that there were "two large wounds on his head and the cranium much broken." This fits the percipient's description that she saw Jakob "with his face all covered with blood." The river is shallow and flows over sharp rocks of lava that must have caused the severe head injuries. A girl working at the sanatorium and returning home from a dance in the middle of the night had briefly met Jakob. He said he had got out of his room through the window. As he disappeared into the darkness, he asked the girl to give greetings to his wife.

The cause of death was known in 79% of our cases and verified by checking official records at the University of Iceland. In 70% of the cases where the cause of death was known, the person had died naturally and in 30% the person had died violently (accident 23.87%, suicide 4.49%, and murder 1.50%). Those who had died by accident, suicide, or murder, were much more likely to be perceived than those who had died by disease. A prominent characteristic of apparitions of the dead is the relatively large number of people who died violently: a much higher percentage than of those who actually die violently in the population.

Stevenson had earlier found that the mode of death was violent in 28% of the cases in which the cause of death was known. These findings raise important questions: Do apparitions of those who suffer a violent death have an invasive character?

The cases of violent death show some interesting and striking characteristics that seem not to have been duly recognized. Also, encounters with people suffering a violent death seem more independent of the relationship to the percipient than do apparitions of those who die naturally.

Another prominent characteristic of reported encounters with the dead is how often they appear close to the time of death. In 14% of the cases in which the time of death is known, the encounter is reported to have taken place within 24 hours before and 24 hours after the time of death. In half of these cases (7%), they were reported to have occurred within an hour of the time of death. Even more startling is the finding that in 86% of the cases occurring within 24 hours of death, the person who had the encounter did not know that the perceived person had died or was dying. In the cases occurring within an hour of death, this figure increases to 89%. Here are two cases:

> My wife and I had living with us a little girl about two and a half years old whom we fostered. One night I woke up and felt as though a woman were standing beside the bed. She said to me, "my name is Margret." Then she vanished out [through] the door. I looked at the clock and saw that it was exactly three-thirty. The day after or the same day I learned that the girl's grandmother had died at that same minute, from a heart attack at Hvammstangi (a town in another part of the country). Her name was Margret. I knew nothing about her health, am not even sure I remembered her name. I had never seen her when she was living.

The wife of the percipient told us that her husband had told her about his experience immediately the following morning and before they had learned of Margret's demise.

The next encounter was reported by a well-known member of parliament in Iceland:

> I was a member of parliament for 18 years and during that time I came in contact with many men who later became good acquaintances. One of them was Karl Kristjansson. We were friends and kept in touch on and off after we retired. One winter's day I went out to the stable as I usually did after lunch. When I had been shoveling for a while, I suddenly felt Karl Kristjansson standing in front of me in one of the stalls in the stable and he said something rather peculiar: "You were lucky, you did fine," and that was all; then he disappeared. That evening his death was announced on the radio. While pondering about the incident and trying to figure it out, I learned that he had suffered a heart attack and been brought to the Reykjavik City Hospital where he died. I had been admitted to that hospital a year earlier after suffering a similar attack. Luckily I recuperated and could go home, whereas he died. In that context I understood his words, "You were lucky, you had good luck."

In half of the encounters (167), another person was present, and in 85 instances, a second person was in a position that should have allowed them to perceive the apparition (e.g., awake, turned in the proper direction). Thirty-nine of these 84 respondents reported that the person who was present shared their experience. Seven of these 39 secondary observers had died and two could not be traced. That left us with 30 witnesses whom we were able to interview. In three cases the witnesses did not remember the incident or refused an interview, and in six cases it was not clear or doubtful whether the new testimony should be considered confirmatory, or whether it was referring to the same incident. However, in 21 instances out of the 30, the witnesses verified the respondent's description of the case.

In the next example, two people report seeing an apparition of the same person at the same time:

> I was around twenty. My father and I sat in the kitchen around noon. Then I saw clearly a woman coming towards us. I was not going to mention it but noticed that my father also saw this. I asked him what he was looking at and he replied, "Surely the same as you." Then he said he knew this woman. She had died a while back. Three or four hours later there was a phone call for my father who was a clergyman. The husband of the deceased woman we saw had died. We had seen the woman around the time her husband had died.

We interviewed the father of the respondent, who described the incident to us and thus verified his daughter's account.

Below is the case of a young man who was seen by more than two people at a time when he was living in a far away part of the country. However, two people did not see the apparition at exactly the same time and place.

I was skating on ice when I felt I saw my friend Erik. I thought this was some nonsense and skated on. A little later I saw him again and close to me, and thought again this cannot be and I must be hallucinating and try to shake it off. I felt a strange feeling going through my body and I looked behind and saw his face. Then I felt sure he must have died. I went home and told them. They said of course that I was talking nonsense. The next morning there came a telegram announcing his death. We did not have a telephone.

Erik had been living at a tuberculosis sanatorium where he died at the age of sixteen. When we asked the percipient's half-sister, Thora, she remembered that her brother had looked shocked when he had come home and told them that Erik had come, he had seen him, and that he had looked pale and miserable. Thora thus certified that the primary witness had told her about his experience before Erik's death was known. Thora told us that some other people had also seen Erik more than once after the incident, although it was never more than one person at the same time. One incident that she experienced herself is particularly interesting:

This happened in the winter. The sheep were out in the valley. I rounded them up and wanted to drive them into the barn. Whatever I did they did not go in and ran to the side. Then I saw where Erik was standing in the doorway. With his arm he pointed west to the farm where his mother was living. Erik then disappeared and I was able to get the sheep into the barn. Later in the winter his mother died of tuberculosis.

A close scrutiny of the cases reveals that collective observations often do not take place at exactly the same time. This is exemplified by the case below, reported by a well-known attorney in Iceland. It still seems reasonable to consider such a case collective.

It was just after graduation in 1939. I was coming home from a dance. I hadn't tasted a drop of alcohol. It was about four o'clock in the morning and full light as we were in the middle of summer. I was walking over a bare hill on my way home from town. Then there came a woman towards me, kind of stooping, with a shawl over her head. And I didn't pay any attention to her but as she passed me I said "good morning" or something like that. She didn't say anything. Then I noticed that she had changed her course and followed me a bit behind. I got slightly uneasy about this, and found it odd. When I stopped, she stopped also. I started saying my prayers in my mind to calm myself. When I came close to home she disappeared. I lived in a house on the compound of a psychiatric hospital where my father worked. I went up to my room. My brother Agnar woke up and said, half asleep, "What is this old woman doing here? Why is this old woman with you?" And I told him not to speak such nonsense but to continue sleeping, although I knew what he meant. I did not see the woman at that time but my brother appeared to see her when he woke up. I went out to get me some coffee. When I returned to my room, Agnar got up again and said, "Why has this woman come back?" And I told him not to act like that, that there was no woman in here, [and] that he was confused and should go to sleep.

At lunch the following day I said to my brother, "What nonsense was this last night? You thought you saw a woman in our bedroom."

"Yes," he said, "I felt as though an old woman came with you into the room." Then our father became attentive and said to me "Did you see something last night?" I told him that I had seen this woman. "That is strange," he said, "around three o'clock this morning old Vigga died." What I had seen fitted her description perfectly.

We approached the respondent's brother. He reported that he remembered this incident and that his brother had told him what he had seen. When asked whether he had seen the woman himself, he replied, "I saw a vague image of a hag ... but not clearly. When I woke up there I saw a woman come in with him. ... This was a patient and always kept inside, I think, if it was her."

The crucial questions are: Where do these intrusions come from? Who initiates these "shadows of the dead"? Some of our cases point to an active role for the deceased person; for example, cases involving persons who have suffered a violent death. The best cases have features that seem to be best explained by accepting some form of survival, as the surveys clearly show. Others may argue that these experiences originate in the mind of the perceiver and that no external agency is needed to explain them. Such interpretations seem cumbersome in view of some of the presented data.

Here I want to end with a personal account. A friend of mine, a scholar, became sick with a difficult and long-lasting disease; he had to stop working and stay in the hospital. He knew of my interest in the question of survival that we had sometimes discussed. A few evenings before he died I visited him and we had a long discussion. Two or three days later I received a phone call in the morning and was told that he had taken his life. He had thrown himself out of a high floor in the hospital. It was a violent death.

After lunch that day I had a nap as I usually do. Just as I was falling asleep or as I started sleeping I felt that my friend came to me, as if alive. I said to him: "What is this? I thought you were dead." Then he stretched his shoulder towards me as if inviting me to touch it. I did and he was solid and in the flesh. Then he disappeared as suddenly as he had appeared and I was wide-awake. He looked serious and appeared face to face with me. His face did not look quite as it used to be and his hair was stained, tangled and disorderly, perhaps from the injuries he must have sustained as he fell on the concrete below.

What was this? A dream most people would think or hypnogogic imagery. Could this be something more? The experience was extremely clear, started suddenly and was very vivid. It was over just as suddenly as if my friend's energy was depleted once he got his message to me. I could not help the feeling that my friend had thrust himself through to my consciousness to show me that he still lived. That was his message to me. This reminded me of how Hafsteinn and his entourage thrust himself through at the funeral of his wife.

This was not the end of it. Often after that, when I was about to fall asleep or waking up, it was as if he came to me. I somehow perceived that he wanted me to talk to his wife whom I had met only at his funeral. This happened in the morning and at night for a few days in a row. I felt that I had to do something and called her. Then it turned out that I could help her with a particular task and that I did.

14

CHILDREN WHO CLAIM MEMORIES OF PAST LIVES

~

I an Stevenson was interested in memories from a past life that some children maintained they had. He started investigating them in the 1960s and quickly learned about numerous cases in various parts of the world. He started his research in India and then investigated cases in other countries, including Sri Lanka, Thailand, Burma, Turkey, Lebanon, and South America. A few cases were also found in Europe.

We learnt about a case here in Iceland. It concerned a boy, who grew up in Reykjavik with his single mother and grandparents. His parents had never lived together and there was very little connection between them. When the boy reached around three years of age, he started talking a great deal about life in the countryside and said that he wanted to see his real mother in the country. He stated that there had been a tractor accident in which a man had died. He mentioned a cowshed and a barn. The boy talked about an older brother and an older man who limped and he mimicked how he limped. He talked about a fire breaking out on the farm and about a boat that had broken.

The boy's father was from the western part of the country. He had had a half-brother who had died at a young age in a tractor accident. He had been driving the tractor between farms when it turned over on a bend in the road and he died immediately. On the farm there was a boat that had been well shielded for the winter, but in a great storm the covering ripped open and the boat was damaged. It also turned out that on the farm there was indeed an old man who limped. It was not uncommon that old people limped at this time, and on every farm there was a cowshed and a barn, so that did not say much either. The boy also mentioned an unusually shaped mountain above the farm, but many farms in this country are located at the foot of a mountain. However, this was not a typical mountain for that area, so perhaps there was something to the boy's story.

Stevenson asked me to interview the boy and his family. He found the incident interesting for it had many of the characteristics had observed in other cases. For example, there had been a fatal accident, which is common in childhood memories. In fact it was not quite clear whether the boy had been a witness to the accident or if he had had the accident himself. Also, it was typical that the boy maintained that he had another mother and wanted to get to his "real" home.

I went and interviewed the boy, his mother, and his father. A long time later, Stevenson came to Iceland and we went to [the] Westfjords and visited the farm where his father came from. The case was not particularly noteworthy, but interesting. Stevenson wrote about it in his book, *European Cases of the Reincarnation Type* that was published in 2003.

This was just before I started my work for the University of Iceland in 1974. In the late 1980s, Stevenson wanted some independent researchers to investigate a few cases to see if they would get comparable results. Stevenson asked me if I was willing to be a part of that project. I was, but on the condition that I could investigate a large enough group of children to do a psychological study of them, with appropriate tests, and compare them with children of the same age who claimed no past life memories. I wanted to know if they differed psychologically from other children.

At this time, Stevenson had been investigating these cases for many years, had written many scholarly articles about them, and had published a few books with his renowned thoroughness and accuracy.

In research such as this it is necessary to have assistants and interpreters, so it is easier to undertake the research in one country. Stevenson agreed for me to do my research in Sri Lanka, where he had already found and researched many cases. It helped that I had been there and liked it more than in India, which I was getting tired of after numerous trips. Stevenson would take care of the expenses, at least at first. I planned to find around thirty cases and assumed that would take a few years.

It was a great help that Stevenson had a group of assistants in Sri Lanka who helped him to find children who claimed to remember past lives. In Sri Lanka, news reporters in the countryside sometimes write reports, when they hear of such children, and send them to their newspapers in Colombo, the capital of the country. This is not something that people feel a need to hide because in Sri Lanka two thirds of the people are Buddhist and many more are Hindus. Rebirth is accepted in their religious tradition, although not everybody there, just like here in Western countries, believes the dogmas of the religion they grew up with. About one fifth of the nation is Christian or Muslim and they generally do not believe in reincarnation.

The reporters often interviewed the children and their parents. Prior to the interview, sometimes no one had been found who fitted the child's description of the past life. After the publication some family might come forth and find a similarity between the report and somebody they had known. That is how some of the incidents were investigated. Most of the cases were from Buddhist families, but there were also a few from Christian families and, occasionally, Muslims.

I started that project in 1988. Initially I chose a different interpreter from the one that Stevenson had had, who had no familiarity with any cases. He was a recently retired official of the ministry of agriculture. The first information about the incidents got to us in three ways: Firstly, from newspaper articles; Stevenson's assistants searched for the articles. Secondly, people contacted the assistants directly and told them about new cases. Thirdly, while we were investigating one case, we were told of another. In Sri Lanka we found on average four to five cases a year.

How did we investigate alleged memories from a past life? At first, interviews were conducted with the parents of the child and then with the child itself about what the child had said that was interpreted as memories of a past life. Often we obtained additional information from grandparents, siblings, and playmates. We would interview one person at a time and let them tell us what they had heard the child talk about. We tried to find as many people as possible who claimed to have witnessed what a child had said about its past life. We then compared the testimony. Was there consistency in what the child had been saying? Had the child talked about these memories for some time, not just once and then only a few words?

Soon I came across some interesting cases, but for many of them, no individual was found who fitted the child's description and had died before the child was born. Sometimes these alleged memories were so general that there was no way to trace a potential previous personality. Sometimes the statements of the children were detailed and quite specific. Two things helped us. The children sometimes reported where they had lived, not by exact street names but by towns or districts. The other thing was that they frequently talked about how they had died and what led to their death. It was particularly noteworthy how many of them described their mode of death. Often the core of their description was what led to their death as if those were the last memories of their past life.

Thusita Silva was a poor girl who lived in the town of Panadura near the west coast of Sri Lanka. At two and a half years of age, she said she had lived in a town called Akuressa. That town was a great deal further south and inland and is far away from Panadura. She said that she and her family had lived in a big house with a pedestrian bridge over a river close by. One day she was walking over the bridge, when she fell into the river and drowned. Her husband threw himself into the river and almost drowned himself. She also said that she had been five months pregnant and her father's name had been Jedin Nanayakkara. This was remarkable to hear from a child not yet three years of age. Her family lived far away from Akuressa and did not have any connection to that town. Finally, her brother, who is considerably older, went to Akuressa and could not find anything to support the girl's account. The girl was scolded for her talk.

We heard about this incident, met the girl and her mother, and were allowed to hear from them what the girl felt she remembered. By this time she was eight years old. We then went to Akuressa, which is 125 km from Panadura and seemed to be a town of around twenty thousand people. We looked for a walking bridge over the river that runs through Akuressa. We found one bridge and asked in the neighborhood whether anyone had fallen off the bridge and drowned. We got the answer that a young girl had fallen into the river and drowned quite a few years ago. We also asked if a family lived nearby with the name of Nanayakkara. Yes, such a family lived near the bridge. We went there.

The house of the Nanayakkara family was large and well painted. The girl had said that the family house was just by the river, a big house and well painted, but in Panadura the girl lived in a small clay hut that was not painted. We knocked at the door of the house of the Nanayakkara family and asked whether they knew about a girl who had drowned in the river. Yes, their daughter-in-law had drowned in the river quite a number of years ago. She and her husband had been on their way across the river, when she fell into the river and drowned. She had been five months pregnant. Her husband, who still lived in the house, had thrown himself into the river to try to save his wife. He almost drowned. This course of events and circumstances were quite unique. Thusita's memories of her past life fitted perfectly with the events of the life of a woman who died a few years before Thusita was born. That became what we called a "solved" case. Could it be that the report of the girl and the events in Akuressa did fit by sheer coincidence? That seems extremely unlikely.

Violent deaths are officially recorded in Sri Lanka, like in most countries. A particular official handles it. His office had a record of the drowning. The woman's name was Chandra Nanayakkara and she was pregnant when she drowned. The child had mentioned that her father's name was Jedin Nanayakkara, but Nanayakkara was, in fact, her father-in-law. Later I found out that it is the custom in Sri Lanka that when a girl marries, she leaves her family and takes on the family of her husband. She calls her father-in-law her father after that. The girl had said his name was Jedin Nanayakkara, but in fact his name was Edwin Nanayakkara. Edwin is a British name, a remnant of British rule in Sri Lanka, which then was named Ceylon. Now this name is disappearing; the girl had apparently not known it and perhaps the name became Jedin from the name Edwin. The names were much alike anyway.

Two things were not verified or were wrong. The girl had said that she had a yellow bicycle, but nobody we spoke to remembered that. She also said that she had worked in a hospital, but she did not. Her best friend had worked in a hospital. Most of her statements about her death and the local surroundings were correct. This was a unique case and we were able to verify it before anybody else did.

15

TWO REMARKABLE CASES

~

Of the 64 cases I investigated in Sri Lanka, 42 remained unsolved, 22 were solved and among them were seven impressive cases. The following case is one of them.

Purnima Ekanayake lived in the town of Bakamuna, which is in the middle of Sri Lanka and quite far north. When she was between two and three years of age, she started saying that she had died in an accident with a motor vehicle. A large vehicle had driven over her. Purnima also said that she and her family had made incense. She had been a man, she claimed; she gave the name of the man's wife and added that he had had two wives.

Purnima said nothing about where this accident had happened until one evening when the family was watching television and there was a documentary about Kelaniya, which is a famous temple not far from Colombo. It is many centuries old and people go there on pilgrimage. The temple stands by a river of the same name. When the family was watching the documentary, Purnima said: "I lived there on the other side of the river."

Around this time a new teacher from the Kelaniya area, by the name of Sumanasiri, came to teach in the school where her father was the principal. Sumanasiri worked at the school during the week, but went home to Kelaniya on weekends. After learning about Purnima's claims, he went with another man over the river and asked about makers of incense. There had been two of them, they were told. One had stopped working and had become an alcoholic, but the other was the member of a family that produced incense. Sumanasiri went there and met a man by the name of Wijesiri, who was making incense. He had had a colleague by the name of Jinadasa Perera. They had run a workshop together and had married each other's sisters. Sumanasiri asked what brand of incense they produced. They made incense that they called Ambiga and Gita Pitcha, and that was exactly what Purnima had said. Wijesiri's friend and brother-in-law, Jinadasa, was run over by a bus on his way to the market. One wheel of the bus went over his chest and he died instantly. The bus driver was sued for careless driving.

I obtained permission to see the documents of the case and among them was the autopsy of Jinadasa that showed that the bus had driven diagonally across his chest, breaking his ribs on the left side and puncturing his lungs. Purnima had a cluster of birthmarks in the exact place where Jinadasa's chest was injured.

Such birthmarks are not uncommon in the cases of children who claim past life memories. The children usually explain such marks as wounds they suffered and from which they died. Purnima's case is typical and very interesting. One of the characteristics of these cases is that they often concern sudden, violent death or an untimely death of a young person.

I went twelve times to Sri Lanka and traveled around the country from coast to coast, except for the far north where civil war was going on during most of those years. Luckily, I found a very good and careful driver whose name was Rohana. He drove me around the country on all these trips, around 5000 km on each trip. I got to know Sri Lanka well, from lowlands covered with palms, where most of the hotels for tourists are located, to mountains with woods, where it is very common to grow tea, and to the dry lands further north. The cases were found in the countryside as well as in the towns.

Apart from studying individual cases, I compared children who claimed memories of past lives with children who did not have any such memories. I gave questionnaires to their mothers and to the children themselves. In these studies the children had reached eight or nine years of age. It is difficult to find psychological tests for younger children.

Children with past life memories had a greater vocabulary than other children, were better pupils, and were often at the top of their class at school. I administered the Child Behavior checklist, a standardized list of problems that children can have, and symptoms that sometimes can lead to problems or difficulties for the parents or children. The results showed that children with past-life memories had more problems than the comparison group. For example, they were more likely to quarrel, for everything had to be exact and correct; they wanted to discuss matters thoroughly were perfectionists; were, rather neurotic;

they had more moods swings and were more prone to nightmares. They also had a stronger temper than the comparison group.

The children had signs of posttraumatic stress disorder and symptoms of children who had experienced violence or had been badly treated. We found no indication that the child had been badly treated in his present life. However, it was quite prominent in their memories that many of them had suffered a violent, sudden death. They had been preoccupied by these memories, talked a lot about them, and seemed to repeat them over and over in their minds. The stress symptoms appeared to be connected to the memories. The question was whether these symptoms had occurred because of the memories of a trauma from a previous life.

It is quite common for these children to suffer from phobias that are connected to their memories of deaths in their past lives. If they talked about having drowned, then they were afraid of wells, sea or lakes. Psychological testing of this kind on children with past life memories had not been done before. The results of this comparison were very interesting and noteworthy. Stevenson had done extensive research on children with memories from a past life and he had noticed various symptoms of this kind, but he had not done a systematic psychological study of them.

Another thing that characterized these cases was that the events which they described occurred within a recent previous lifetime in Sri Lanka. The events were never related to lives that had occurred hundreds of years ago or in foreign countries.

I published articles about my psychological studies in academic journals: the *Journal of Nervous and Mental*

Disease (1995), the *Journal of Scientific Exploration* (1997), *Transcultural Psychology* (2000), and *Psychology and Psychotherapy: Theory, Research and Practice* (2003).

The BBC in collaboration with CBS in the U. S. got me to cooperate in making a documentary on a few cases. The documentary was called "In Search of the Dead" and Jeffrey Iverson produced it. He had earlier written a widely read book, *More Lives Than One.*

Channel Four in Britain followed with a documentary on Purnima Ekanayake. Finally Storyhouse Productions in Washington made yet another documentary about my work. They spared no expense, emphasized beautiful filming, and it was shown far and wide, such as on the Discovery Channel, on ProSieben in Germany, and in many places in Asia.

After several years working on cases of children with past life memories in Sri Lanka, I decided it was time for a change, and went to Lebanon, where I studied 30 cases among the Druze, a Middle Eastern religious group that believe in reincarnation. I published articles that thoroughly described four cases. One of these cases was truly extraordinary: the case of the boy Nazih al-Danaf.

When very young Nazih started , saying that in his previous he had carried two pistols and four hand grenades and had been fully equipped with weapons. He said that he had been an adult, had owned a house and had children. Armed men had come; there was an exchange of fire, and he was killed. Nazih gave the name of the town where he had lived; he wanted to go home to fetch his weapons. He had also said that he had a deaf friend, and that his wife was more beautiful than his present mother. He said there was a cave near his house and mentioned other things as well.

His parents did not pay attention to this for quite a while. He had many siblings. I interviewed Nazih's parents and siblings, one at a time. All of them had heard his claims. Nazih said he had lived in Kabershamun, which is a small town about 17 km distant from his home. Eventually the family gave in and took him there. When they had reached the main crossroads of the town's center, he told them to take the next road to the left, then to turn left into another road and drive to the end of that road. There they stopped and the boy ran up a steep road to the left, with his father after him. That was where he was supposed to have lived.

Meanwhile his mother and sister stayed at the car. A young man by the lowest house on the steep road was washing his car. He started talking to them and asked what they were looking for. They told him that Nazih claimed he had lived on this road in a past life and was looking for his house and his family. They related Nazih's statements about his past life. The young man said that they fit his father, who had died many years before. He asked the boy's age and called his mother, who was working in a field close by. Then Nazih and his father, who had both run further up the road, came back down the road and towards the house.

A widow lived there with her two teenage children. It turned out that her husband had died in fighting during the Lebanese civil war. He had been a bodyguard of the leader of the Druze in Lebanon and also had been the office manager at their headquarters in Beirut. One night men broke into the headquarters, killed two guards at the security gate, made their way into the house, where her husband was shot dead. His name was Fuad Khaddage.

At first the widow was very skeptical and questioned Nazih closely. For example, who had built the gate to the house? Nazih answered correctly. She also asked whether she had had an accident while they lived in Ainab, which was not far away. He answered that she had dislocated her shoulder, which was correct. She asked him whether their daughter had become ill and he answered that she had become seriously ill from taking medicine that belonged to him.

Then Nazih asked: "where is the barrel that I used when I taught you how to shoot?" She showed them a rusty barrel was in the garden that her husband had used when he taught her how to shoot. She invited Nazih into the house. He said he wanted his weapons and walked to a cupboard in one of the rooms where they had been kept, but they were no longer there. The family had let go of the weapons after Fuad's death. His widow explained this to my interpreter, Majd Abu-Izzeddin, and me. Everything Nazigh said proved true and Fuad's widow was convinced that he was her husband reborn.

Fuad Khaddage had a brother, who was alive, and Nazih was taken to his home. The brother, Sheik Adeeb, also wanted to test the boy and asked how he could prove that he had been his brother. Nazih answered: "I gave you a gun." The brother asked what kind of a gun. "It was Czech sixteen." That was correct. Sheik Adeeb asked the boy to tell him where he, as Fuad, had lived with his first wife. Nazih asked him to come with him up the road. They walked quite a way up the road. There, Nazih stopped, pointed first to a house and said that his father had lived there. Then he pointed to the next house. There he had had lived with his first wife, he said. Fuad Khaddage had been married twice and had divorced his first wife.

Later Sheik Adeeb went to visit Nazih, laid a revolver on the table, and asked whether this was the gun he had given him. The boy looked at the gun and said: "No." That was correct. Everything the boy said to Fuad's widow and to Sheik Adeeb was correct.

The warm relationship between Nazih and his former family was obvious and continued to be so.

How did Nazih's 22 statements about his former life fit the facts of Fuad Khaddage's life? All that could be proven right or wrong were correct. There was only one doubtful statement. Nazih had said that he had received an anesthetic injection in the arm when he was driven in the ambulance to the hospital. Fuad was shot in the head at close range and must have died immediately. It is therefore difficult to understand why he was given an anesthetic injection, but not out of the question.

It seems that Nazih was quite a rowdy child, even unruly. Majd Abuzzeddin and I had the name of his father and the name of the road where he lived, but no road number, as is common in Arabic countries, where houses are often without a number. We therefore asked for directions in a store. We were asked why we wanted to talk to the man's son. Then the clerk asked: "What has he now done?"

The case of Nazih is almost too good to be true. I spent much time interviewing the witnesses, but to no avail. All statements that could be tested proved correct. In this incident I did not find people or places myself, as I did in Akuressa. The case on the other hand makes use of testimony of various witnesses whom I interviewed thoroughly. I could not find anything that did not fit in their stories, however much I tried. I wrote a long article on this case in the *Journal of Scientific Exploration* (2002).

National surveys show that about one fifth of Europeans believe in reincarnation. The incidence of the belief varies by country. The surveys also show that about half of those who believe in life after death believe that they will be born again. The idea of reincarnation is not only well-grounded in Buddhism and Hinduism, but has considerable following among Christians. I wrote an article on research that explores these views in various countries in Europe. It was published in *Nordic Psychology* in 2006.

16

THE PHYSICAL MEDIUM INDRIDI INDRIDASON AND THE FIRE IN COPENHAGEN

~

I n the year 1759, Emanuel Swedenborg described in the presence of witnesses in Gothenburg, a fire that broken out near his home in Stockholm, nearly five hundred kilometers away. There were fifteen witnesses present. Three days later the first messenger arrived from Stockholm to Gothenburg with news of a great fire in Sodermalm in Stockholm. The fire was described in newspapers and the course of events matched the description that Swedenborg had given of his vision. Swedenborg lived in the eighteenth century, was a famous scientist, and a member of The Swedish Academy of Sciences.

News of this account spread far and wide in its time. Among the people who heard of it was Immanuel Kant, the famous German philosopher. Kant felt that the account was amazing and he got a friend of his, a

British merchant, who sometimes went to Stockholm and Gothenburg on business, to meet the witnesses and examine the account. The messenger returned to Kant with a positive report that is, unfortunately, lost. However, there exists a letter that Kant sent to a friend of his, where he relates the incident and writes that it is impossible to explain in the conventional way. He writes in the letter that there's no doubt this account is true.

A similar example describing events that happened far away is found in the sources and diary entrances of a séance that was held with Indridi Indridason on the 24th of November 1905. Indridi Indridason had come to Reykjavik as a young man to learn printing and stayed with his uncle. Around this time, Einar H. Kvaran and his friends started experimenting with séances in the hope of producing spiritistic phenomena but with few results. On one occasion, when the meeting was held at the home where young Indridi stayed, he was invited to the meeting. He had barely sat down, when the table moved with such a jolt that Indridi became afraid and wanted to leave the meeting.

Strange phenomena started happening in these meetings whenever Indridi was present. It seemed he was endowed with unique mediumistic talents. Lengthy records of séances describe events that took place in detail; these were written down both by Einar Kvaran and Haraldur Nielsson, a professor of theology. Indridi is by far the most important Icelandic medium and one of the most important in the history of Spiritualism.

Things would move around Indridi even though two sitters held his hands and feet to avoid any suggestion of fraud. Gudmundur Hannesson, a professor of medicine, wanted to examine Indridi's phenomena thoroughly. He strung a net right across the meeting room from the floor to the ceiling so that Indridi was the only one inside the net, apart from Haraldur Nielsson, who held his hands. Gudmundur stood by the only opening of the net to ensure that no one could get in or out. In spite of this, things started moving outside the net and no "normal" explanation was to be found. Not only did objects move, they flew around the room. Some of these objects were musical instruments and they played as they flew around outside the net, some distance from Indridi. The séances were held in darkness, because that was the only way physical phenomena could be seen. Gudmundur Hannesson glued fluorescent ribbons on the objects, so that they could more easily be seen in the darkness, and a dim light was briefly lit occasionally. Some phenomena also happened in full light. Not only were objects raised off the ground, but also Indridi himself sometimes levitated. He flew or glided in the air and sitters had difficulty holding him down.

Among the amazing phenomena around Indridi – to put it mildly – were that voices were sometimes heard around, which appeared not to come from his own vocal chords. At Indridi's sittings, a voice that sounded like the soprano voice of a trained female opera singer was sometimes heard. The sitters named her the French singer for she spoke in French. Idridi didn't speak French. Another voice, a very deep one, also appeared at the meetings and they sometimes sang duo. Indridi was a good singer, but it was out of the question for him to sing a duo or in a female soprano voice. Brynjolfur Thorlaksson, who was the organist at the Reykjavik Cathedral, was one of the sitters at these séances. He affirmed that none of the guests at the meetings could have sung that well.

One occasion, several voices were heard quarrelling. The name Malibran was mentioned, which the French female singer claimed to be. Those who were present looked up the name Malibran in encyclopedias. Malibran was one of the most famous opera singers in the world during the early part of the nineteenth century. Her first names were Maria Felicia. She was from a family of singers and her father had been the favourite tenor voice of the composer Rossini. She died in 1836 at only 28 years when she fell off a horse. Bear in mind that the communicator Malibran was coming through Indridi in 1905, seventy years later.

At one sitting, a man appeared in a pillar of light. He introduced himself as Mr. Jensen. He said that during a break in the meeting he had gone to Copenhagen. A factory in the city had caught fire. Jensen first appeared at the meeting at nine o'clock in the evening, then disappeared and came back at around ten o'clock and told the sitters about the fire. An hour later he said that the fire brigade had been able to extinguish the blaze.

In those days there were neither telephone nor radio contact with Iceland. News from abroad arrived only by ship, sometimes the following day. Einar Kvaran and Haraldur Nielsson duly recorded the Jensen communication. This time they also went to Bishop Hallgrimur Sveinsson and wrote down what had happened so that the bishop could be a witness to the event if it turned out to be true. A document was left with him. The bishop was a subscriber of the *Politiken*, Denmark's largest newspaper.

Close to Christmas, a ship arrived from Denmark with copies of the *Politiken*. On the 25th of November there was news of a fire in a factory in Copenhagen. People had become aware of the fire around midnight in a factory in Store Kongensgade 63. There was a two hour and fifteen minutes time difference between

Iceland and Denmark at this time, which meant that the time frame fitted Jensen's arrival at Indridi's meeting. Everything Jensen had said turned out to be true – the timing, that there had been a fire in a factory, and that the fire brigade managed to put it out in one hour.

Logbooks were kept of Indridi's sittings, where everything that happened at the séances was written down. Most of these logbooks are lost. Only one exists and it starts with a séance on the 11th December 1905, just after Jensen appeared for the first time and talked about the fire in Copenhagen.

In the logbook we find that Jensen appeared again at a séance on the 11th of December 1905. There he introduced himself for the first time with his first name Emil. It appears that the sitters asked him some questions about himself. He said that he had no children, had been single and died when he was not so young. He had siblings who were still living. After this event, Jensen became quite a frequent guest at Indridi's meetings.

Nobody had bothered to search for evidence of whether this Jensen had, in fact, existed. Now that his full name was known and some information of his life, I wanted to find out whether this man could to be found in Danish documents and if what he had told about himself was correct. Jensen is a very common surname and Emil is quite common as well.

I looked for him at the National Archives in Copenhagen. In the census of 1885, I found an Emil Jensen. He had been an owner of a factory, and it was made clear both by Kvaran and Nielsson that Emil had referred to himself as a *fabrikant*, which is Danish for a factory owner. In *Köbenhavn's Vejviser*, it turned out that there was only one fabrikant named Emil Jensen and, to my great surprise, he lived at Store Kongensgade 67, two houses along from number 63, where the fire had taken place.

Census records also showed that Emil Jensen was born in Amaliegade, but his family moved to Store Kongensgade 40, which was close by. There his father, and later Emil, ran a shop for decades. Jensen was last recorded as living in Fredericagade 16 that crossed Store Kongensgade close to where the fire was. Jensen had, in fact, lived all his life in this area.

I found out various other things about him. He had lived with his four sisters and none of them married. His full name had been Thomas Emil Jensen, but he never used the name Thomas. I was also able to trace his death certificate. He had died in 1898, at fifty years of age, which was not considered particularly young in those days. His sisters and his two brothers all died after him. Everything matched what Jensen/Indridi had said at the sitting of 11th of December 1905, when Emil Jensen talked about his life.

I also checked how frequent fires had been in Copenhagen at that time. Four fires had taken place in four weeks around the date of the fire in Store Kongensgade, but that one was the only fire that happened at the time of the sitting in Iceland. The fire was also the largest, the only one that happened around midnight, and the only one that had occurred in a factory in the four-week timeframe.

This is an important case and compares equally with the case when Swedenborg described the fire in Stockholm. In the case of Swedenborg, he seems to experience this himself from afar, but in the case of Indridi, a deceased person (Jensen) at a sitting with Indridi describes the event. It seems absolutely impossible to explain this event in any normal physical way. With the technology of that time it was not possible to send any quick messages between Reykjavik and Copenhagen.

People were so impressed by Indridi's phenomena that they formed The Experimental Society to study him. A special house was built for the activities. It had an apartment for Indridi so that he could be available full time. Many important people and academics were members. Gudmundur Hannesson, a professor of medicine, asked for permission to study Indridi. His research was so extensive and thorough that it could not easily be improved now, if we exclude the light-sensitive equipment that is now available to record what takes place in the darkness.

Gudmundur followed Indridi for a whole winter and wrote articles about his observations between 1910-1911. They were translated into English and appeared in the *Journal of The American Society for Psychical Research* in 1924. Nielsson gave lectures on Indridi at World Congresses on Psychical Research, which were held in Copenhagen and Warsaw in the 1920s. Kvaran wrote a great deal about Indridi and his phenomena.

It would take too long to list all the phenomena witnessed by numerous sitters that happened at the Indridi sittings as described in the logbooks. Knocks responding to the sitters' questions were often heard coming from walls. . Sometimes a swift gust of wind went through the hall and people were blown about. A scent or other smells for which the source could not be determined might arise. Lights appeared in various colors, or there was a column of light in which beings appeared. Deceased people (if that's what they were) would appear next to Indridi, side by side with him, or people would appear suddenly in different parts the hall, but only for a short time.

At some of the meetings, hands or feet or even a single finger appeared. People were touched by invisible hands or could touch them in the dark. While all this was going on, a guard, who held Indridi's hands and put his leg over Indridi's leg, carefully watched him. Sometimes there were two guards, one on each side. Often people's clothes were pulled and objects thrown around the room. Frequently, voices which didn't appear to come from the sitters or Indridi were heard elsewhere in the hall. Some were voices of people who had been known while alive to individual sitters, and they were able to converse with them. Sometimes the sitter talked to old friends who had passed away, and the voice of the deceased, as well as their way of talking, was the same as it had been while they were living. Yet, Gudmundur Hannesson writes in one logbook, what was said more or less blended with the thoughts of the medium or was like him. Sometimes special "proof meetings" were held, where the deceased told of incidents in their lives or described things that they had owned. For example, the widow of a deceased man was asked to go through a list of things, which he claimed had belonged to him. She knew almost everything that he had described. These sittings were very convincing for the sitters, who often went on to become Spiritualists. In other words, they became convinced that they had communicated with the departed, and convinced that we survive physical death.

Before Indridi, Spiritualism was almost unknown in Iceland.

Indridi had his opponents and critics, but they were mostly among religious fanatics or sceptical people who had never witnessed the phenomena that took place at The Experimental Society. Indridi was studied for only five years. In 1909 he became ill with tuberculosis and died at Vifilstadir hospital on the 31st of August, 1912. He was just 28 years old. Kvaran met him 24 hours before he died. By that time he had become so weak that he could barely speak. Indridi told him that he knew of and saw his departed friends. "His certainty of them," writes Kvaran about their last meeting "was just as clear as his certainty of me."

Loftur Gissurarson and I authored a biography of Indridi titled *Indridi Indridason: The Icelandic Physical Medium.* It was published by White Crow Books in 2015 and has received excellent reviews.

17

RESEARCH AND TEACHING AT THE UNIVERSITY OF ICELAND

~

Sigurjon Bjornsson had been appointed a professor to organize studies for a B.A. in psychology at the University of Iceland We got along well and shared an interest in conducting research. Sigurjon was resourceful in obtaining research funds for us. He was a Freudian psychoanalyst and worked with Wolfgang Edelstein, who had been brought up in Iceland but lived in Berlin, where he was the director of the Max Planck Institute for Education and School Research (Bildungsforschung).

In 1976, the Faculty of Social Sciences was founded by bringing together sociology, psychology, political science, teaching studies, librarianship and social work. We had many faculty meetings since various regulations and decisions had to be made. This took a lot of time and some colleagues were quite talkative; too much in my view. Prominent at these meeting was the professor for political science, Olafur Ragnar Grimsson, who later became the President of Iceland.

Once, after a faculty meeting, I was walking with Olafur Ragnar between two buildings of the university. There something strange happened. Suddenly I felt as if the man walking beside me was wearing armor from centuries ago. The armor rattled. I felt it covered only his upper body and shoulders and was made of small, light iron plates that shook when he walked. I had never seen or heard of such armor. I almost said to Olafur Ragnar, "stay still" so I could "feel" him better, but I restrained myself. I felt that he had been a leader at a time of revolt and armed rebellion, and the country where he had been living was close to collapsing, as in a civil war. There was something very Cromwellian about this. At the same time I almost said to him: "You will become a head of state, even at an international level", but I restrained myself and stayed silent.

This incident is truly memorable and I did not tell a soul about it until much later, when I told a colleague in sociology. What happens when such images come by force into the mind, as if they were a vision? Do hidden dimensions of the mind cast up images and words to explain cause and effect – in this case the personality of Olafur Ragnar? Is it possible that time loosens its boundaries of past and future, so that a greater reality appears? Concerning the future, it has long since come true, for Olafur Ragnar Grimsson became the president of Iceland and was reelected several times. As far as the past is concerned, there is no way to prove it. I can add thought, that after some research, I found out that light armor consisting of small plates has existed in the past.

At this time, Olafur Ragnar belonged to a small leftist party and there was no indication that he would ever become our president. Generally, Olafur and I seldom spoke to one another and we were quite different. Perhaps he came into this life with an important past, equipping him with leadership qualities and an ambition for a position of power.

Someone may ask if I have often sensed the far past of a person. Aside from Olafur I don't recall that, except for a glimpse of my own past, which I have already described. It is noteworthy that both in the case of Olafur Ragnar and myself, we find a successful revolt (Olafur) and a fatal revolt (me).

My time at the University of Iceland was productive and peaceful with only occasional frictions, some regarding the selection of new faculty members. This, I assume, is common in universities.

At times I did not agree with the majority of my faculty. In spite of that I enjoyed enough confidence among my colleagues that they trusted me with important positions, such as a membership of the grant-giving committee. The rector (president) of the university, Sigmundur Gudbjarnarson, started some new policies and research became more important. A committee was appointed in each department to evaluate if a faculty member's research was sufficient for promotion to a higher position. I was made the chairman of the progress committee within the faculty of social sciences.

The time came when I was to get a promotion to a professorship. A few individuals criticized the research I was doing. They talked to deaf ears. The University Council approved my promotion by ten votes; two were against, and one abstained. In 1979 I was promoted to associate professor (docent). The Council agreed unanimously.

Our rector, Sigmundur, strengthened the Research Fund of the university. We had to get applications evaluated by qualified people. After that the committee decided if a grant should be given and how high. I enjoyed this position and I learned a great deal about research at the university.

In 1980 the Parapsychological Association held its annual convention at the University of Iceland. Over one hundred participants attended and it involved a lot of work for me.

Several students worked with me on my research projects and some have remained good friends up to the present day; friends such as Loftur Reimar Gissurarson, who completed his doctorate in Edinburgh. I published academic papers with several of my students. I emphasized research and publishing papers in peer-reviewed journals, now over seventy in number.

I taught courses on psychological testing, methodology and research methods, and two other optional courses. One was on parapsychology and the other on states of consciousness, such as sleep, dreams, hypnosis, multiple personality, and religious experiences.

In 1993 I was offered the post of visiting professor for a year at the *Institut fuer Grenzgebiete der Psychologie und Psychohygiene* in Freiburg that Professor Hans Bender had established. I was invited to do any research I pleased. I obtained one-year leave of absence and found a capable person to replace me. I was offered an additional year in Freiburg and was granted one more year leave of absence.

When I returned home two years later intending to teach my usual courses, another man had been employed to teach them without informing me, so I was not able to teach the minimum required number of courses. That was an unpleasant situation. I started thinking that it was time to retire, three years before it became obligatory. I retired on the 1st of February, 1999. I kept my office until I reached seventy, and received some research funds and travel stipends during that time.

In hindsight, my "forced" retirement proved to be beneficial. It gave me more time to devote myself to my interests and research. I was able to spend more time at the University of Virginia, where I was always welcome. I was regularly invited to give lectures abroad (and still am). One thing is certain. My time at the University of Iceland was enjoyable and productive and I am grateful for having had the opportunity to work there for almost three decades.

18

COMPANIONS AND CONTEMPORARIES

~

M argret passed away in 2005. After that I started travelling even more than before and sometimes I stayed at the University of Virginia for two to three months at a time. Stevenson and his wife had moved to a home for the elderly and offered me the use of their house. After Stevenson became confined to bed, I visited him from time to time. By coincidence, I was present with his wife and brother when he passed away peacefully on the 8th of February, 2007, at 88 years of age. He was one of my mentors and may have influenced me more than anyone else.

Stevenson was of Scottish descent and born in Canada, where his father had been a journalist for *The Times* of London, *The Scotsman* and The *New York Times*. His father sent him to secondary school in England and after that he studied medicine at McGill University in Montreal. He soon became an active scholar and a researcher in the field of conventional medicine. Later, he also turned towards less conventional projects, such as children's alleged memories of a past life. He became a pioneer in that field. I wrote an obituary about this great friend and mentor.

Requests for lectures increased; the most I gave was in 2010, more than 30 on three continents and in fourteen countries, including Brazil, Argentina and Hong Kong. When the invitation came from Hong Kong, I took the opportunity to travel to Tibet; I had wanted to visit Tibet for many years, perhaps since my twenties, after reading with great interest Walter Evans-Wentz's translation of Tibetan scriptures, now more commonly known as *The Tibetan Book of the Dead*.

Because of the political situation and unrest due to the Chinese domination and suppression, travelling to or around Tibet wasn't straightforward. We had to go with a tourist operator and anywhere we wanted to visit had to be planned in advance and permissions obtained to visit the various places. Sometimes the country was closed for tourists. At that time, to reinforce their hold of Tibet, the Chinese government lured more and more Chinese to Tibet, offering various favors, such as low taxes.

I took three travel companions with me: friends from Austria. I was particularly interested in visiting the monasteries that have been the great religious and educational institutions for centuries. Now they are a shadow of what they once were. A significant number of monks, including the Dalai Lama, have fled to India where they have rebuilt most of the leading monasteries. Early in my youth, in my mind, I had clear images – as if from a past life – of great mountainous scenery as if I were looking across a wide valley and seeing high mountains on the other side. During my visit to Tibet, I sometimes wondered if I would come to face this scenery again. I didn't.

All my life I have enjoyed my work and spent much of my time working. Yet, I also have had my hobbies and enjoyed them when I had the time. In 1987 I bought a piece of land in the Laugardal valley in the south of Iceland where my father was born. My father and sister came with me to select the lot. My father was not able to see the summerhouse that I had built there in the spring of 1988, for he died on the 26th of March that year. Later, I bought additional pieces of land on both sides of the summerhouse, so I had three lots, side by side, and plenty of space.

I started growing trees and got myself a small greenhouse. Now, my land has many tall trees of various kinds. Sometimes I have been too enthusiastic and the young trees have become too numerous, so I've given them to friends and acquaintances. Recently I gave 300 trees to the Dalbui golf course by Middalur in memory of my grandfather, Erlendur Thorleifsson, a farmer at Ketilvellir. He was buried in the Middalur church graveyard. There is also quite a grove of my trees east of the Hekla volcano around the summerhouse of my friend, the meteorologist Thor Jakobsson and his wife Johanna. Others have enjoyed my trees including Arnor Hannibalsson in the Kjos and Loftur Reimar Gissurarson in Mosfellsbaer, both long time friends.

Thorgrimur Gudmundsson, called Toggi, is my first cousin, and he has done things for me from time to time, particularly when I've been abroad. He is a former policeman and former head of the police association. Since the retirement of his brother Sigurdur, we often meet and have a meal together at the University cafeteria. Sigurdur is my age, and the former managing director of the Icelandic department of housing. He studied history and is now working on his doctorate. I would also like to mention my favourite aunts, Gudrun and Gudny, on my mother's side and Inga on my father's side. Skuli Alexandersson, former Member of Parliament, was married to an aunt of mine and I visited them from time to time. Both have now passed away. He was very knowledgeable about the area around the Snaefellsjokull glacier.

My mother's brother, Olafur Elimundarsson, completed a master's degree in history in his older years. He wrote a three-volume history of the area north and west of the Snaefellsjokull glacier. I travelled many times with him in this area, and learnt to appreciate the majestic landscape and its history, which has now been made a national park, and for a good reason. There my forefathers lived by fishing under difficult conditions and the women would give birth without any help. I particularly remember the ruins at Einarslon that stand above a steep cliff by the sea.

My uncle Olafur Elimundarsson died before he could fully complete and publish his second and third volume on the history of this area. My relative Gudmundur Saemundsson, Skuli Alexandersson and I completed it, and the University Press published it. Heimir Gislason is a cousin of mine, who lives in Hellissandur and I try to visit him every year.

I have good friends on both sides of the Atlantic Ocean. In the U.S. there are Emily and Ed Kelly, the late Robert Van de Castle, who ran the Institute of Sleep and Dream Research at the Department of Psychiatry at the University of Virginia. Jeffrey Hopkins is a respected Tibet scholar at the University of Virginia; he has edited books by the Dalai Lama and worked as his interpreter. The psychiatrists Bruce Greyson and Jim Tucker are Stevenson's successors, both productive and highly respected researchers. Carlos Alvarado, now in Durham, I have known for decades. We first met in the 1980s at the early Parapsychological Association conventions when he was an assistant to Dr. Stevenson. Carlos is a great scholar and highly knowledgeable of early psychical research.

I should also like to thank journalist, Leslie Kean, who kindly wrote the foreword to this book, and Jim Matlock, who co-authored my most recent book, *I Saw A Light And Came Here.*

I lecture more often in the UK than in any other country. There I know the unique historian Andreas Sommer at Churchill College in Cambridge, the active group at the University of Northampton, in particular Chris Roe and Callum Cooper, the unbeatable Tricia Robertson in Glasgow, and my publisher Jon Beecher, who travelled with me to India in 2013 and has visited me in Iceland with his lady, Nadine, and we travelled around together.

In Freiburg, Germany, I have had friends for decades. Eberhard Bauer is at the Institut fuür Grenzgebiete der Psychologie und Psychohygiene that I visit regularly. In Freiburg I usually stay with my long time friends Ulrich and Heidrun Timm. These three have all visited Iceland.

Then there is Gesa Dröge in Germany, who has helped me so much over the years.

I must mention my late friend and colleague Martin Johnson from Lund University. He became professor of parapsychology at the University of Utrecht in Holland, the only Chair in parapsychology in Europe. We worked closely together and conducted a series of experiments on the relationship between ESP performance and perceptual defensiveness.

Here I must mention, again, my daughter, Anna Elisabeth, who carries the name of my loving mother from Hellissandur. Her husband is Frank Topitsch and their children are Max Jonatan and Nils Benjamin. They live close to Heidelberg and I follow what is going on in their lives. I visit them as often as I can, which always gives me great joy. We often chat over the phone. Anna was brought up in Germany. She has a PhD in mechanical engineering.

Finally, last but not least, I must mention my son, Haraldur. He was born in 1956 to my first wife, Helga Haraldsdottir, who was Icelandic. Our interests are in many ways alike. He is a medical doctor, a psychiatrist, and lived for many years in England with his former wife Svanhildur and their children Helgi, Logi and Eik. Now they have all, with the exception of Logi, moved back to Iceland. Haraldur Erlendsson, is now the doctor in charge of the entire south coast of Iceland and I am very proud of him. All these people have enriched my life.

19

LOOKING FORWARD TO
THE UNKNOWN

~

L ife has treated me gently. I have been lucky; met people who led me further to what interested me, and so easily that, at times, it looked as if I was being led. Probably these are coincidences, but one can ponder, are all coincidences really random events? Of course, we cannot tell. I have also speculated whether my present life is a continuation of a distant past life.

I have met some fine people who were very supportive of me, both while studying and at work. Here I think of Hans Bender, Joseph Banks Rhine, Ian Stevenson, and Karlis Osis, who all were outstanding in their respective fields. I have sometimes referred to them as "my masters" or mentors.

I was not a particularly good student and was often interested in things other than those I was supposed to concentrate on at the time. In high school, I was interested in astronomy and religion. At the university in Freiburg, I was busy with Kurdish affairs. But I managed to stay the course and had the strength to complete what I intended to accomplish.

It is very fortunate to be born into circumstances that make it possible to choose. That should not be taken for granted. A large portion of humanity lives in circumstances that give them little or no choice; they are stuck in circumstances they cannot get out of.

I was lucky to be born in a country where there is freedom and security. Here, people disagree about politics and express themselves with words, without using weapons or violence. I was fortunate to have a fine father, who was intellectually inquisitive, and to be brought up in a community with an opportunity for education.

Early in life I was moulded by philosophy and became fascinated by the question of reality: what is real and what is the real reality, if I may phrase it so. Consciousness and its apparent ephemeral nature has always been a key question. Where is and what is our consciousness while we sleep? Can it be that we are draped with the veil of forgetfulness, when we awake and that our consciousness during sleep is active in another reality?

According to Plato – if I still remember this correctly – the basis of consciousness is beyond time and space. We come into this world of the senses and we gradually become enmeshed in it. If that really is so, it is prudent to suppose an existence before this one, and a life after physical death. However, the circumspect Plato also ponders if the soul (consciousness) is like a tune that is played on the harp. If a string of the harp is damaged it is not possible to play and the soul no longer exists. One can read between the lines that Plato rather supports the alternative view and then he usually points to Pythagoras.

We are a species named *Homo sapiens,* or the man of wisdom and knowledge, for a good reason, but we are nevertheless the man of ignorance. We are not much closer to understanding what really exists than the ancient Greeks were, although science has made a giant leap forward in understanding what is physically real but, in the end, there is always an unknown.

For at least two to three thousand years, religious writings—Christian, Hindu, Buddhist—and mythology have maintained that continued life waits for us after physical death. This is the religious tradition. Then science came along and men started to look to nature for answers. Science developed quickly and people increasingly started to doubt the value of the religious traditions. By the latter part of the nineteenth century, a separation had formed between religion and science, particularly after Darwin's theory appeared on the scene. Fierce, loud debates developed between science and religion.

It became clear how important research was in all areas. Research alone could provide reliable knowledge. Ways were found to study the phenomena of spiritism and mediumship that appeared around the middle of the nineteenth century; also phenomena like poltergeists, alleged encounters with the dead, and various psychic phenomena. This became known as psychical research, and British scientists were in the forefront.

Psychical researchers looked at themselves as scientists, for they used scientific methods.

Are there scientific arguments for the afterlife? Let us first look at the question: what is the main argument against the afterlife or life without the physical body? Consciousness has biological foundations. Mental maturity changes drastically from birth to the years of an adult, along with the growth of the body and the brain and also often later in old age. Various illnesses, particularly in the brain, can cause major changes to the mind. Some medications and chemicals can cause hallucinations, make us unconscious and make consciousness disappear. These are strong arguments against an afterlife, as they show a strong correlation between the brain and consciousness and point to consciousness being a result of brain function.

Let us look at the other side; what – if any – are the scientific arguments for the afterlife?

First, let us mention physical deterioration. Sometimes it happens that people who seem to be out of touch with reality, for example because of dementia, Alzheimer's, and vascular or schizophrenia of the most serious kind, seem to become lucid shortly before their death. It's known as terminal lucidity. Having not been lucid, sometimes for years, they suddenly recognize their loved ones and talk to them rationally as if they have recovered; then they usually pass away.

In 2012 I co-authored an article "terminal lucidity" with colleagues, Bruce Grayson and Michael Nahm, which has been published in the journal, *Archives of Gerontology and Geriatrics.*

There's also the argument that some people have of visionary experiences of those who have died. Why do people sometimes become aware of people whom they did not know had passed away and often at the exact time of the person's death?

Why do some people sometimes sense dead people so well that they can describe them? Why are these departed people sometimes later found to be connected to the place where they were seen? Why is there often a purpose for the visions, e.g. to save someone from imminent danger?

Then, there are visions that many people have close to the time of death, which I have mentioned in my books; deathbed visions. Why do some people, as they are dying, sense a loved one who has died, who has come to "collect" them? After this experience they often die in a state of serenity.

Then there are the people who find themselves outside of their physical body during a cardiac arrest or some other life threatening event: the so-called near-death experience.

Sometimes people sense those who have passed away around them, similar to the deathbed visions. People sometimes see a light or beings of light and a tunnel, which they go through and, at the same time, they sense that they are separate from their body and therefore not their body. These events are life changing for many of those that have them because they conclude that they are more than their physical bodies. Even hardcore atheists are changed as their worldview collapses as a result of the experience.

Then there is mediumship. Sometimes those who have passed away describe events in their life, that neither the medium nor others present had any possibility of knowing. Such was the case of Emil Jensen and the fire in Copenhagen, and other events I've mentioned in this book. Can we put all these events down to delusion and coincidence? There is so much data now that it's difficult to take that view. These phenomena are at least *indications* of continued life after death or something beyond the five senses.

Some have argued that the one who has the experience creates it himself in his own mind. Those explanations are complicated and, in my view, unlikely. One could also add some religious experiences, where people experience within their soul, unity with divine power. Many of those who have these experiences can never doubt the existence of a spiritual reality that is beyond or woven together with the material world.

Finally, there are the children who claim memories of a past life. Sometimes, information about individual from the past life they are describing can be found and details from that life are validated. Often, the previous life ended violently or because of an accident.

It is as if psychological symptoms caused by a difficult death experience follow them into this life. Many of these children start talking about their past life memories as soon as they are able to talk and some carry scars or birthmarks, matching injuries that led to their death in a past life.

All these arguments for and against have come about through research. That is a great step forward from the time when only religious arguments existed.

Now, many will ask, where is this reality where the departed live and what is it like? Few things can be said about that here, except that presumably it is first and foremost of a mental nature. Is it one of the "multiverses" that William James first proposed as an idea? Now cosmologists discuss multiverses, although they differ from William James' multiverses. The cosmologist and astronomer Bernard Carr, professor at the University of London, recently wrote a book on multiverses. He accepts the possibility that a spiritual world could be one of these worlds.

Since my early youth, one *credo* has remained solidly ingrained in me: purity of body and purity of mind bring us closer to the True, the Good and the Beautiful. Then, there is also within me the doubting Thomas, the scientist, who checks on me, who is skeptical and will accept nothing but the truth.

In my youth when I had the "lightful experience" and others that followed, I entered into a prayer-like approach to the Great Presence that at times overwhelmed me. This Great Presence can be so overwhelming that it shakes us like a straw in the wind. Is that the Ultimate Unknown, the Being in which we live, and of which we are perhaps a tiny part without knowing it? Is that the Spirit of Planet Earth?

Whatever it is, I am grateful for having had the opportunity to participate in the mystery of life for the past eighty-eight years. One day I will part with the physical body that my parents gave me. Then some sadness may occur for leaving loved ones behind. Whenever that will be and wherever I may go, I look forward to getting closer to the Unknown.

EPILOGUE

~

I have never felt so sad to lose someone in parapsychology as I have felt in losing Erlendur Haraldsson. I first encountered him in August 1979 at the Parapsychological Association Convention, which took place at St. Mary's College, Moraga, California.

At the time I was a master's degree student in the parapsychology program at John F. Kennedy University, California, under the supervision of John Palmer. John was also the President and organizer of the Parapsychological Association convention and I was one of the students recruited by him to help in its organization. I still remember seeing Erlendur, tall and impressive, walking toward the convention rooms. He did not know who I was, but I was extremely impressed by his elegant and generous attitude toward others.

I have always admired his interest in many areas of parapsychology. Few scientists in the field have covered as much ground as he did, particularly when it comes to experimental research and spontaneous cases. I have always felt that his contributions to the investigation of mediumship and deathbed visions are particularly important and remind us of the evidence for survival of death. This is evident in his bibliography, which contains numerous wide-ranging studies, too extensive to mention here.

Erlendur's studies of deathbed visions, with Karlis Osis, which took place in the USA and India in the 1970s resulting in their book, At the Hour of Death (Avon Books, 1977 and later editions), were particularly important and are still cited today.

Erlendur also conducted investigations of apparitions of the dead, particularly in his native Iceland. That research is summarized in his book The Departed Among the Living: An Investigative Study of Afterlife Encounters (White Crow Books, 2012).

Equally important is his study with Ian Stevenson of the Icelandic Medium Hafsteinn Björnsson: "The Case of Runolfur Runolfsson," which he writes about in a previous chapter. He once said of Stevenson, "For me it was a great learning experience to work with Stevenson, to plan the research we did together ... and to get acquainted with the thoroughness of his inquiries, his skillful art of interviewing witnesses, and his interest in improving methods for the study of mediums ..."

His studies with mediums contributed greatly to rescue this topic for careful scientific exploration.

Erlendur conducted studies of historic mediums, in particular, the Icelandic physical medium, Indridi Indridason. His extensive research into Indridason resulted in his book Indridi Indridason the Icelandic Physical Medium, co-authored with Loftur R. Gissurarson (White Crow Books, 2015). I enjoyed the book immensely and was honored when Erlendur asked me to write the introduction.

He also contributed important studies of children who claimed to remember previous lives. That work was summarized in his book, I Saw a Light and Came Here: Children's Experiences of Reincarnation, co-authored with James G. Matlock (White Crow Books, 2017).

Although I first saw Erlendur in 1979, we met again in the early 1980s when I was working at the University of Virginia as a research assistant to Ian Stevenson. A good friend to Erlendur, Stevenson assigned me to help him to finish his book about the Indian guru, Sathya Sai Baba. Erlendur asked me to find cases in the spiritualistic and psychical research literature of phenomena similar to those produced by Sai Baba. It was fascinating to hear him talking about the phenomena that Baba appeared to produce in Erlendur's presence, none of which Erlendur could explain by conventional means. Eventually that work was published in his book "Miracles are My Visiting Cards": An Investigative Report on Psychic Phenomena Associated with Sri Sathya Sai Baba (Century-Hutchinson, 1987). In 2013, two years after Sai Baba's death, the book was revised and expanded under the title Modern Miracles: The Story of Sathya Sai Baba: A Modern Day Prophet (White Crow Books, 2013).

A little while later, Erlendur returned to the US and we continued to have long discussions. I learned much from him (back then I was new in the field) and he once told me that he saw me as a colleague, not as an assistant. This was one of the most satisfying moments of my early career in psychical research.

In later years, when he visited us again in Charlottesville, he stayed with me and my wife, Nancy Zingrone, and used one of my cars. He also stayed with us briefly after we moved to Virginia Beach. He took us out to dinner a few times and we had many conversations, not only about parapsychology, but also about his life.

Although he conducted a great deal of research showing that ESP was related to psychological variables in the laboratory, I feel that one of Erlendur's greatest contribution was to expand the importance of seeing the phenomena outside the confining experimental lab walls. Without rejecting laboratory work, he reminded us of personal experiences, the phenomena of mediums, and of the richness and implications of powerful experiences such as deathbed visions apparitions and, later, recollections of previous lives.

Erlendur stated that he was greatly influenced by scientists in the field such as J.B. Rhine, Karlis Osis, and Ian Stevenson. I think that many of us, myself included, were also positively influenced by Erlendur, both personally and professionally.

Although we used to email each other frequently, the communication stopped last year. He told me in an email sent on December 15, 2019: "I am well, but have become unsteady on my feet; 88 now." The loss of his frequent contact was inestimable. He was so influential on my life and work and for that I will be forever grateful to him.

Carlos S. Alvarado,
North Carolina,
December, 2020

REFERENCES

~

Glipmses and Touches

Erlendur Haraldsson (1964). *Med uppreisnarmonnum i Kurdistan*. Hafnarfjordur, Iceland:

Skuggsja.

Erlendur Haraldsson (1967). *Land im Aufstand Kurdistan*. Hamburg: Matari Verlag.

Erlendur Haraldsson (1972). *Vasomotorische Reaktionen als Indikatoren aussersinnlicher Wahrnehmung*. Inaugural-Dissertation zur Erlangung der Doktorwürde der Philosophischen Fakultäten der Albert-Ludwigs-Universitaet zu Freiburg.

With J. B. Rhine In Durham

Erlendur Haraldsson (1972). Psychological variables in GESP test using plethysmograph recordings. *Proceedings of the Parapsychological Association, 7,* 6-7.

Erlendur Haraldsson (1972). Precognition of a quantum process. A modified replication. *Proceedings of the Parapsychological Association, 7,* 71-73.

With Ian Stevenson at the University of Virginia

Erlendur Haraldsson and Ian Stevenson (1975). A communicator of the "drop in" type in Iceland: The case of Runolfur Runolfsson. *Journal of the American Society for Psychical Research, 69,* 33-59.

Erlendur Haraldsson and Ian Stevenson (1975). A communicator of the "drop in" type in Iceland: The case of Gudni Magnusson. *Journal of the American Society for Psychical Research, 69,* 245-261

Karlis Osis And The American Society For Psychical Research in New York.

Karlis Osis and Erlendur Haraldsson (1977). Deathbed observations by physicians and nurses: A cross-cultural survey. *Journal of the American Society for Psychical Research, 71,* 237-259.

Karlis Osis and Erlendur Haraldsson (1977). *At the hour of death.* New York: Avon Books.

The Medium Hafsteinn Bjornsson

Erlendur Haraldsson and Ian Stevenson (1974). An experiment with the Icelandic medium Hafsteinn Björnsson. *Journal of the American Society for Psychical Research, 68,* 192-202.

Erlendur Haraldsson, J.G. Pratt and Magnus Kristjansson (1978). Further experiments with the Icelandic medium Hafsteinn Bjornsson. *Journal of the American Society for Psychical Research, 72*, 339-347.

Speaking In A Foreign Language – A Case of Xenoglossy

Erlendur Haraldsson (2017). A Rare Case of Mediumistic Xenoglossy. Paranormal Review (in print).

Visions Of The Dying Among Americans And Indians

Erlendur Haraldsson (1999). Obituary: Karlis Osis. *Journal of the Society for Psychical Research, 63*(854), 127-128.

Of This World And Another In Iceland

Erlendur Haraldsson and Joop M. Houtkooper (1991). Psychic Experiences in the Multinational Human Values Study. *Journal of the American Society for Psychical Research.* 85(2), 145-165.

Erlendur Haraldsson and Orn Olafsson (1980). A survey of psychic healing in Iceland. *The Christian Parapsychologist, 3*, 276-79.

Erlendur Haraldsson (2006). Popular psychology, belief in life after death and reincarnation in the Nordic countries, Western and Eastern Europe. Nordic Psychology, 58(2), 171-180.

Erlendur Haraldsson (2011). Psychic experiences – third of a century apart. Two representative surveys in Iceland. *Journal of the Society for Psychical Research*, 75, 903, 76-90.

Face To Face With Sathya Sai Baba, "The Man Of Miracles

Erlendur Haraldsson and Karlis Osis (1977). The appearance and disappearance of objects in the presence of Sri Sathya Sai Baba. *Journal of the American Society for Psychical Research, 71*, 33-43.

Karlis Osis and Erlendur Haraldsson (1979). Parapsychological phenomena associated with Sri Sathya Sai Baba. *The Christian Parapsychologist, 3*, 159-163.

Erlendur Haraldsson (1987). *"Miracles are my visiting cards. An investigative report on psychic phenomena associated with Sri Sathya Sai Baba."* London: Century-Hutchinson.

Erlendur Haraldsson (1988). *Modern Miracles. An investigative report on psychic phenomena associated with Sri Sathya Sai Baba.* New York: Ballantine Books. (USA edition of "Miracles are my visiting cards.").

Bilocation and Changing Water into Petrol

Karlis Osis and Erlendur Haraldsson (1976). Out-of-body experiences in Indian swamis: Sri Sathya Sai Baba and Dadaji. *Research in Parapsychology 1975*, Metcuhen, N. J.: Scarecrow Press, 147-50.

Experiments on Healing and Precognition

Erlendur Haraldsson and Thorsteinn Thorsteinsson (1973). Psychokinetic effects on yeast. An exploratory experiment. *Research in Parapsychology 1972*, Metuchen, N. J.: Scarecrow Press, 20-21.

Erlendur Haraldsson (1994). Research on alternative therapies in Iceland. In H. Johannessen, L. Launsö, S. G. Olesen & F. Staugård (Eds.), *Studies in alternative therapy 1* (pp. 46-50) Gylling, Denmark: Odense University Press.

Erlendur Haraldsson (1980). *Scoring in a precognition test as a function of the frequency of reading on psychical phenomena and belief in ESP*. University of Utrecht: Research Letter, Parapsychology Laboratory, 1-8.

Children Who Claim Memories of Past Lives

Antonia Mills, Erlendur Haraldsson, & H. H. Jurgen Keil (1994). Replication studies of cases suggestive of reincarnation by three independent investigators. *Journal of the American Society for Psychical Research.* 88, 207-219.

Erlendur Haraldsson and Godwin Samararatne (1999). Children who speak of memories of a previous life as a Buddhist monk: Three new cases. *Journal of the Society for Psychical Research, 63*(857), 268-291.

Erlendur Haraldsson (2000). Birthmarks and claims of previous life memories II. The case of Chatura Karunaratne. *Journal of the Society for Psychical Research.* 64(859), 82-92.

Erlendur Haraldsson and Majd Abu-Izzeddin (2002). Development of Certainty about the Correct Deceased Person in a Case of the Reincarnation Type in Lebanon: The Case of Nazih Al-Danaf. *Journal of Scientific Exploration.* 16(3), 363-380.

Erlendur Haraldsson (2003). Children who speak of past-life experiences: Is there a psychological explanation? *Psychology and Psychotherapy: Theory Research and Practice. 76,* 1, 55-67.

Erlendur Haraldsson (2012). Cases of the Reincarnation Type and the Mind-Brain Relationship. In A. Moreira Almeida and F. S. Santon (ed.). *"Exploring the Frontiers of the Mind-Brain Relationship."* New York: Springer. 215-231.

Erlendur Haraldsson (2001). Do Some Children Remember Fragments Of A Previous Life? In Lorimer, D. (Ed.). *Thinking beyond the brain.* London: Floris Books, 81-94.

Erlendur Haraldsson and Jim Matlock (2017): *I Saw a Light and Came Here* (White Crow Books).

Erlendur Haraldsson (2006). Popular psychology, belief in life after death and reincarnation in the Nordic countries, Western and Eastern Europe. Nordic Psychology, 58(2), 171-180.

Two remarkable Cases

Erlendur Haraldsson and Godwin Samararatne (1999). Children who speak of memories of a previous life as a Buddhist monk: Three new cases. *Journal of the Society for Psychical Research, 63*(857), 268-291.

Erlendur Haraldsson (2000). Birthmarks and claims of previous life memories I. The case of Purnima Ekanayake. *Journal of the Society for Psychical Research, 64(858),* 16-25.

Erlendur Haraldsson. (1997). Psychological comparison between ordinary children and those who claim previous-life memories. *Journal of Scientific Exploration*, 11, 323-335.

The Departed Among the Living

Erlendur Haraldsson (1988-89). Survey of claimed encounters with the dead. *Omega, the Journal of Death and Dying, 19*(2), 103-113.

Erlendur Haraldsson (2009). Alleged Encounters with the Dead. The Importance of Violent Death in 337 New Cases. *Journal of Parapsychology.* 73, 91-118.

Erlendur Haraldsson (2012). The *Departed Among the Living. An Investigative Study of Afterlife Encounters.* USA and UK: White Crow Books.

The Physical Medium Indridi Indridason and The Fire In Copenhagen

Loftur R. Gissurarson and Erlendur Haraldsson (1989). The Icelandic Physical Medium Indridi Indridason. *Proceedings of the Society for Psychical Research, 57,* 53-148.

Erlendur Haraldsson (2011). A Perfect Case? Emil Jensen in the mediumship of Indridi Indridason. The fire in Copenhagen on November 24th 1905 and the discovery of Jensen's identity. *Proceedings of the Society for Psychical Research,* 59(223), 195-223.

Erlendur Haraldsson and Johan L. F. Gerding (2010). Fire in Copenhagen and Stockholm. Indridason's and Swedenborg's 'Remote Viewing' Experiences. *Journal of Scientific Exploration.* 24, 425-436.

Erlendur Haraldsson (2012). Further facets of Indridi Indridason's mediumship; including 'transcendental' music, direct speech, xenoglossy, light phenomena, etc. *Journal of the Society for Psychical Research,* 76(908), 129-149.

Erlendur Haraldsson and Loftur R. Gissurarson (2015). Indridi Indridason the Icelandic Physical Medium. UK and USA: White Crow Books.

Companions And Contemporaries

Erlendur Haraldsson (2008). Obituary: Ian Stevenson (1918-2007). *Journal of Parapsychology.* 71, 159-168.

Erlendur Haraldsson (2008). At the deathbed of Ian Stevenson. *Journal of the Society for Psychical Research.* 72(893), 255-256.

Erlendur Haraldsson (1999). Obituary: Karlis Osis. *Journal of the Society for Psychical Research,* 63(854), 127-128.

Erlendur Haraldsson (1978). ESP and the Defense Mechanism Test (DMT). A further validation. *European Journal of Parapsychology,* 2, 104-114.

Erlendur Haraldsson and Martin Johnson (1980). ESP and the Defense Mechanism Test (DMT): A case of experimenter effect? *Research in Parapsychology 1979.* Metuchen, N. J.: Scarecrow Press, 112-113.

Erlendur Haraldsson & Joop Houtkooper (1995). Meta-analysis of ten experiments on perceptual defensiveness and ESP: ESP scoring patterns, experimenter and decline effects.. *Journal of Parapsychology,* 59(3) 251-271.

Looking Forward To the Unknown

Michael Nahm, Bruce Greyson, Emily Williams Kelly, Erlendur Haraldsson (2012). Terminal lucidity: A review and a case collection. *Archives of Gerontology and Geriatrics* 55, 138–142.

Many of my papers can be downloaded from my homepage www.hi.is/~erlendur and from ResearchGate. net.

Epilogue

(E. Haraldsson, "Ian Stevenson's Contributions to the Study of Mediumship." *Journal of Scientific Exploration,* 2008, 22, 64–72, p. 68).

Some parts of this chapter appeared in my blog: Erlendur Haraldsson (1931-2020) https://carlossalvarado.wordpress. com/2020/11/24/erlendur-haraldsson-1931-2020/

ACKNOWLEDGEMENTS

~

O ne day a prominent political scientist, historian and colleague, Hannes Holmsteinn *Gissurarson* told me that a publisher wanted me to write my biography. It had never occurred to me to write one. I replied after some thought, I will write up a list of chapters. But then the publisher must get someone to interview me about each of them and write up the essence of these interviews. This was done by Haflidi Helgason, whom I had never met before. He visited me twice a week, we chatted for an hour or two, and he brought back a short text, which I revised and expanded. A few months later the book was published by Almenna bokafelagid (Jonas Sigurgeirsson) and sold about nine hundred copies.

Then, a lovely lady Bjorg Jakobsdottir entered my life. She on her own initiative – with no encouragement from me, started to translate the book. She worked on it slowly but steadily and finished it around the time I completed writing *Indridi Indridason, The Icelandic Physical Medium.*

This was a chance to review my life again at the age of eighty-five. I revised Bjorg's translation, deleted and expanded as I deemed fit for a foreign readership. My British publisher and friend Jonthan Beecher decided to publish it, perhaps as a favor to me.

My heartfelt thanks go to: Bjorg Jakobsdottir, Hannes Holmsteinn Gissurarson, Haflidi Helgason and Jonathan Beecher.

INDEX

A

Adeeb, Sheik, 134-135
Agnar, 117
Akuressa, 125-127, 135
Al-Danaf, Nazih, xii, 132
Alvarado, Carlos, 155, 167
American Psychological
   Association, 20, 22
American Society for
   Psychical Research, 8,
   19-20, 143
Aquino, Thomas, 5
Archives of Gerontology
   and Geriatrics, 160
ASPR, 17, 20-22, 26, 29, 82

B

Bagvantam, S., 65
Banerjee, D. K., 66
Barrett, Sir William, 41
Barzani, Mustafa, 5, 76, 80

Bauer, Eberhard, 155
Beecher, Jon, xiii, 155
Bender, Hans, 5, 6, 10, 16,
   72, 149, 157
Benediktsson, Thorvaldur,
   38
Bjornsson, Sigurjon, 146
Bjornsson, Hafsteinn, 12,
   29, 91, 165, 169, 170
Bjornsson, Jon, 35, 36
Blanda, 108
Brunton, Paul, 2, 71

C

Cooper, Callum, 155
Carlson, Chester, 8, 13
Carr, Bernard, 162
Castle, Robert van de, 10-
   12, 154
Chitravati River, 84-85
Culver, James C., 49

D

Dalai Lama, 152, 155
Deathbed Visions, 17, 19, 21, 27, 41, 49, 91, 161, 164-165, 167
Duke, University, 8-9

E

Eckhart, Meister, 16
Edelstein, Wolfgang, 146
Eiriksson, Gudlaugur, 32
Ekanayake, Purnima, xii, 79, 128, 132
Elimundarsson, Olafur, 154
Emilsson, Tryggvi, 57
Erik, 116
Erlendsson, Haraldur, 68, 156

F

Fanibunda, Dr. Eruk, 66
Farrukabad, 23
Felicia, Maria, 140
Fenwick, Dr. Peter, 49-50
Fleischer, Helga, 18
Franzson, Bjorn, 53
Fredriksen, Svend, 35-38
Fuller, John G., 20
Fylgja, 56

G

Ganges, River, 24
Gardastraeti, 34
Gardner, Martin, 20, 66

Gardur, 32
Geir, 5-6
Gislason, Heimir, 154
Gislason, Magnus, 38
Gissurarson, Loftur, xiii, 22, 145, 149, 153, 165
Glen Ridge, 51
Gokak, V. K., 65, 84
Greeley, Andrew, 55
Grenzgebiete der Psychologie und Psychohygiene, 149, 155
Greyson, Bruce, 155
Grimsson, Olafur Ragnar, 146-147
Gudbjarnarson, Sigmundur, 148
Gudmundsson, Ludvig, 13
Gudmundsson, Sigurdur, 153
Gudmundsson, Thorgrimur, 153
Gullfoss, 21, 27, 72
Gunnell, Terry, 58

H

Hannesson, Gudmundur, 138-139, 143-144
Hannibalsson, Arnor, 153
Haraldsson, Helga, 11, 17, 18, 71
Haraldsson, Anna Elisabeth, 18, 156
Heidegger, Martin, 5

Index

Heinrich, Rombach, 5
Helgadottir, Hulda S., 36
Helgadottir, Thordis, 40
Hjalmtysdottir, Margret, 21, 26-28, 40, 72, 113-114, 151
Hopkins, Jeffrey, 154

I

Icelandic National Library, 34
Indridason, Indridi, x, xiii, 22, 29, 34, 137-138, 145, 165
Ingvar, David, 48-49

J

Jakob, 111-112
Jakobsdottir, Bjorg, 177, 178
Jakobsson, Johanna, 153
Jakobsson, Thor, 153
James, William, 17, 162
Jensen, Emil, xiii-xiv, 140-142, 161
Johnson, Martin, 155
Jonsson, Jon, 13
Journal of Nervous and Mental Disease, 131
Journal of Parapsychology, 9

K

Kabershamun, 133
Khaddage, Fuad, 133-135

Kalimpong, 24
Kanchipuram, 23
Kant, Immanuel, 137-138
Kean, Leslie, xv, 155
Kelaniya, 128-129
Kelly, Ed, 154
Kelly, Emily, 154
Khaddage, Fuad, 133-135
Kidd, James, 19-21
Kjos and Loftur, 153
Köbenhavn
Krishna, Gopal,, 84-86
Kristinsdottir, Gudlaug E., 40
Kristinsson, Hordur, 40
Kristjansson, Karl, 114
Krystal, Sidney, 64
Kumar, Amarendra, 88
Kvaran, Einar H., 34, 138, 140-141, 143, 145

L

Larusdottir, Elinborg, 12, 36-38

M

Malibran 139-140
Mansson, Man, 13
Murphy, Gardner, 20-21

N

Nahm, Michael,, 160
Nanayakkara, Chandra, 126-127

Nanayakkara, Edwin, 126-127

Nanayakkara, Jedin, 126-127

Narasimhaiha, Hosur, 83

Nielsson, Haraldur, 138-141, 143

Nordic Psychology, 136

O

Orlob, 5-6

Osis, Karlis, xii, 8, 16-17, 19, 21-25, 27, 41, 50-51, 59, 72, 78, 157, 165, 167

P

Palmer, John, 52, 164

Perera, Jinadasa, 129

Petursson, Thordur, 38

Phantasms of the Living, 110

Plato, 158

R

Ragnarsson, Ulfur, 36, 38

Randi, James, 66

Rhine, Joseph Banks, 7-11, 22, 77, 91, 157, 167

Robertson, Tricia, 155

Roe, Chris, 155

Rognvaldsson, Sveinn, 38-39

Runki, (Runolfsson, Runolfur), xiii, 12, 14-15, 31, 33, 40, 165

S

Sandgerdi, 13-15, 106

Sathya Sai Baba, 24, 59, 61, 63, 65, 67, 83-91, 166

Schulman, Arnold, 24

Sem-Jacobsen, Carl Wilhelm, 49

Shirdi, 87

Silva, Thusita, 125

Singh, Ranjoth, 88

Society for Psychical Research, 8, 17, 19-20, 22, 34, 51, 143

Society for the Scientific Study of Religion

Sodermalm, 137

Sommer, Andreas, 155

Stefan, 31

Stevenson, Ian, xii, 8, 12-13, 15, 17, 23, 29-30, 42, 77, 112, 121-124, 131, 151, 155, 157, 165-167

Store Kongensgade, 140, 142

Sumanasiri, 129

Surviving Death, xii

Sveinsson, Hallgrimur, 140

Swatos, William, 22

Swedenborg, Emanuel, 137, 142

T

Tanous, Alex, 26

Thompsen, Martinus, 2-3, 71

Thorleifsson, Erlendur, 153
Thorsteinsson, Thorsteinn
Tigrett, Isaac, 87
Timm, Heidrun, 77, 155
Timm, Ulrich, 77, 155
Topitsch-Haraldsson,
    Benjamin, 156
Topitsch-Haraldsson,
    Frank, 18, 156
Topitsch-Haraldsson, Max,
    156
Transcultural Psychology,
    132
Truzzi, Marcello, 66
Tucker, Jim, 155

U

University of Freiburg, xii, 5
University of Iceland, x, xii,
    17, 22, 27, 49, 52, 58, 91,
    112, 123, 146-150
University of Virginia, xii,
    8, 10, 12-13, 15, 77, 150-
    151, 154-155, 166

V

Varadu, 85-86
Venkatagiri, 84, 88-89
Venkatagiri, Raja of, 84-85
Vigga, Old, 118

W

Wijesiri, 129

X

Xerox, 8